A Life Story

A Life Story:
the Poems of
Inge Ginsberg

Collection © 2014

This is a work of fiction. All the characters and events portrayed in this book are either fictitious or are used fictitiously.

Gray Rabbit Publications
1380 East 17 Street, Suite 2233
Brooklyn, New York 11230
www.FantasticBooks.biz

ISBN 10: 1-62755-632-X
ISBN 13: 978-1-62755-632-3

First Edition

Table of Contents

Emotions

Sex and Lovers

Mein Herz

1984 und 2014

Mein braves starkes Herz
Du tapferer, standhafter, kleiner Trommler
Der die Fahne des Lebens verteidigte
In verzweifelten Tagen
Als Hitler's Horden es bedrohten
Unablaessig zur Hoffnung haemmernd.

Du jagtest heisse Wuestenwinde durch die Adern
In einsamen bluetenschweren Naechten
Und galoppiertest freudig
Zu den Hoehen der Liebeserfuellung.

Noch darfst du nicht muede werden
Noch sind unsere Pflichten nicht getan
Haemmere, schlage, bohre, kaempfe
Aber gib nicht auf
DU ARMER, EINSAMER, KLEINER, TAPFERER TROMMLER.

Erdenschwere

New Age, bereits 2.9.71

Erlass Deinem Geist die Erdenschwere
erloes ihn zur Groesse
lass ihn schweben ins Leere
Lass ihn ahnen die Schaetze
von alten Kulturen
in den sterbenden Resten unserer Naturen
Lass ihn schweben
und weben an raren Gedanken
lass ihn um fliehende Wolken sich ranken
Lass ihn lauschen dem Nichts und der Ewigkeit
und spuere dich selbst als einen Teil der Zeit.

Ode an Nini

Swan Lake, Juli 2012

Das Aug' erkennt Auge
Das Hirn sucht sein Hirn
Die Haut passt zur Haut
Wie Harold und Maude.

Was webt in Aeonen
Und plant in Billionen
Ist unser Raum-Zeit
Eine Kleinlichkeit.

Soll lehren und heilen
Soll Frieden verteilen
In Familien und Nationen
Religionen un Generationen.

Bilingual

Weg Genossen

13. Dez 93

Wir gingen eine lange Strecke zusammen
erfolgreich, genussreich
haben wir einander getroestet und gestaerkt
wir haben miteinander
ueberlebt, dank
der Staerke des einen
des Witzes, der Schlauheit und Verstandes
des anderen.
Die Beine und Muskeln des Athleten
haben Berge erklettert
doch der Poet sah die Weite und Hoehe
die Nase fuehlte den Duft
der Luft
doch die Blumen, Kraeuter und Waelder
erfasste der Dichter.
Die starken Arme haben Seen durchschwommen
die Haut fuehlte das Wasser, die Kuehle
der Andere dachte an
Das Urmeer, das Woher und Wohin
Die Lippen haben gekuesst
der Leib hat in Leidenschaft geglueht
die Liebe, die Zaertlichkeit
das Wollen und Koennen
fuehlte der Andere,
Der Mund ass was die Haende bereiteten,
Trost, Staerkung, Ersatz fuer erlittenes Leid
des Anderen.
Bald werden wir uns trennen muessen
Musik und Poesie

Comrades in arms

October 04

We came a long way together,
Seeking and finding pleasures, love, success,
Thanks to the strength of the one
And the quick wit and perception of the other.

We climbed high mountains together,
the athlete sprinting over rocks and stones
Like a mountain goat,
The poet looking into space and time.

We swam in glacier lakes and Caribbean warm seas,
The strong arms dividing the waters,
The poet feeling the primordial soup
we all came from.

We cooked delicious gourmet meals,
together enjoying the emanating scents,
the tickled tastebuds, the colours
that nourish body and soul.

And love—the one never could get enough
kisses, caresses, the passionate ecstasies of bodily lust,
The other forever seeking the trinity
of spirit, body and soul, combined in THE one.

It is heart breaking that sooner or later
they will have to separate,
"partir c'est mourir un peu"
this time it will be "partir c'est mourir pour toujours."

kein Trost mehr
fuer Hunger, Durst und Schmerz.
waehrend langer Jahre
waren wir ein unzertrennliches Team.
Jetzt sind wir beide muede
der Leib wird sicher ruhen
sich aufloesen
wiederkehren im ewigen Rundlauf der Natur.
Was wird aus Dir
arme Seele
ohne den Trost des Leibes
wirst du Ruhe finden im Nichts?
Verloren und vergessen all
das Wunderbare das du
erlernt, erlebt, erfasstest?
Verloescht die Flamme ohne Spur?
Wirst Du, Seele, wandern und wiederkehren
ohne Erinnerung?
"partir c'est mourir un peu"
Dieser letzte Abschied, die trennung von Leib
und Seele
wird "mourir pour toujours".
Schade, denn diese Seele passte in diesen Leib
sie waren gute Weg-Genossen.

Like Michalengelo, who complained
"Oh Lord, why did you put
the soul of a beautiful youth
into mine, a crippled hunchback's body."

My body and soul are a perfect match.
You, my beloved body, will return in the eternal circle of life,
but you "animula pallida," my little fragile soul,
how will you survive without the comfort of physical pleasures?

Will you easily find a new partner
or will you forever be searching?
What a pity that we have to separate, We are
perfect comrades, arm in arm.
And we will try hard to march on together
for a very long time to come.

Oekonomie

Jemand macht die Farben fuer die Fasern
fuer die Bandln
fuer die Mascherln
fuer die Blumerln
die Busenhalter unauffaellig schmuecken.
Wenn diese etwas billiger werden muessen
Eliminiert man natuerlich
die sowieso unauffaelligen
Blumerln und damit die Mascherln
fuer die man dann keine Fasern
fuer die Bandeln und daher auch
keine Farben braucht.
Und der diese Farben machte
kann keinen Cadillac mehr kaufen
ad infinitum

Economics 101

Somebody sells the dye
for the fiber
for the ribbons
to form the tiny flowers
that adorn
almost invisible
the middle of brassieres.

The producers of the dye
and the fiber
and the ribbons
and the flowers
and the bras
buy a Cadillac each every year.

Therefore the automaker and the steelworker
Therefore the tire maker and the rubber worker
Therefore the seat maker and the leather worker
Therefore the lacquer maker and the dye worker
have enough money to buy the bras
with the almost invisibile flowers
for their wives.

One day, the bra producer decides
to reduce expenses, by eliminating
the tiny, almost invisible, flowers.

No more flowers
No more ribbons
No more fibers
No more dye
and no more Cadillacs.

Therefore no money for bras
with or without flowers
for the workers of steel,
for the workers of rubber,
for the workers of leather,
for the workers of dye

et cetera ad infinitum…

Gott Amor ist boshaft

im Central Park 11.Okt.2012

Wenn der Partner passé ist,
und die Beziehung cassee ist
Ist es schade um jedes Wort,
schnuer es zum Paket und wirf es fort.

Wenn Luegen die Liebe ersetzt,
Ausreden das Vertrauen verletzt
Dein Selbstbewusstsein leidet,
ist es besser man scheidet.

Wenn Sachen machen
wichtiger ist als Lachen,
Wenn das Licht im Gesicht
nicht mehr leuchtet,
nur Traenen das Auge befeuchtet
Freude und Glueck saust berg ab,
Cut your loss, schreib's ab.

Winsel nicht um Liebe, bettel nicht um Zeit
Gott Amor ist boshaft,
er freut sich wenn du weinst.
Es ist nicht deine Schuld,
vielleicht fehlt Dir nur Geduld
Was immer es sei, es ist vorbei.

God Amor is Malicious

New York 15.9.2012

If the partnership is passé
And the relationship is cassée
Do not cry out loud
Just throw it out.

If Trivia replace laughter and lust
If foul excuses hurt your trust
If your pride and ego fade like the Cheshire cat
Just leave that rat.

If your faces, when you approach, do not illuminate
if your heart rate does not double
when he is as the gate
it is nobody's fault,
you just lost your hold
your passion turned cold;
offer it to the highest bidder and shout: sold.

Do not whimper and whine
And beg for more time
God Amor is malicious,
he thrives when he can be vicious
be strong and shine,
and start a new love, a new trip, a new rhyme.

Alte Frauen sitzen gern auf Baenken

Tel Aviv, Shderot Chen, Fruehling 2004

Alte Frauen sitzen gern auf Baenken
Womoeglich wo einst ihre Kinder spielten
Dann die Enkel, jetzt haben sie
Nur noch einander und die Erinnerungen
Die sie bindet und die sie
immer wieder wiederholen.

Sie waren in der Haganah zusammen,
schmuggelten Waffen unter ihren Roecken,
als Kinder waren sie bei den Zofim,
und spaeter auf den Universitaeten,

Die eine heiratete den Bruder der anderen,
Die andere stahl den Braeutigam der besten Freudin
kurz vor der Hochzeit.

Jedenfalls schliefen sie alle miteinander
kreuz und quer wie es damals ueblich war
als die Pille auf den Markt kam
Und Penicillin die Furcht vor jeder Krankheit nahm.

Damals waren ihre Schenkel glatt,
die Muender heiss und in den Augen brannte
ohne Scham Einladung und Verlockung zur Lust der Liebe.

Was ich heute sah, sind drei eng aneinander geschmiegte,
fuerchterlich verkrueppelte Gestalten,
Gesichter wie haessliche Masken,
wie man nur im Karneval sie traegt.

Shderot Chen

Spring 2004

Women, when they are really old
Like to sit on benches, squeezing against each other.
They sit on Shderot Chen, under the old trees,
where their children played a long time ago,

Then the grandchildren.
Now they only have each other and the memories they share
Which they resuscitate
again and again and again.

During WW2 they fought together in the Haganah,
Smuggling weapons under their skirts
And breaking the siege,
Either by smiling to the British or creeping behind the lines.

1948 they danced in the streets,
under the newly planted trees on the Shderah,
full of joy and hope
and started normal lives.

One married the brother of the other,
The other stole her best friend's fiancé
two days before the wedding.
But friends they remained.

In the sixties they slept and fucked freely
criss and cross, everybody with anybody
It was the blessed time of the pill, penicillin
and many years before AIDS killed men and pleasure.

Die einst schoenen Frauen sind nicht mehr zu erkennen.
Aber einander sehen sie sich
mit den Augen der Erinnerung,
jung, schoen, eifersuechtig, ehrgeizig,
Und sprechen daruber, immer wieder
Immer wieder…

Their thighs were lithe and smooth,
their bodies kept the promises
of the luring eyes and the burning lips,
those of the mouth and the other ones.

What I see today there on the bench
Squeezing one against the other
to catch some human warmth,
Under the old high trees, on the well kept flowered alley?

I see three horribly distorted bodies, their faces like the frightening masks
Worn in carnival, to chase away bad spirits.
BUT: They see each other in the mirror imprinted with their youth and love.
Three friends, rehashing their memories again and again and again.

Vaya con dios, Kleiner Bruder

Quito, Hotel Quito, Dez. 05

Heute habe ich ein Leben gerettet.
Hilflos lag er auf dem Ruecken,
verzweifelt zappelten seine Beine,
versuchte er, wie Kafka's metamorphosierte Schabe
Sich umzudrehen.
Hoffnungslos schien es,
dass er sein Ambiente,
seine naturbestimmte Umwelt
je wieder sehen werde.

Hat er seinen Hilfeschrei ins Universum gesendet?
Wieso stieg ich gerade jetzt die Stiegen vom Hotel
zum Swimmingpool hinab?
Seit 30 Jahren komme ich in dieses Hotel, mache jeden Morgen mein
Mini Yoga und Baumenergie im Garten.
Niemals noch benuetzte ich diese Stiegen.

Wieso gerade heute, als der braune Kaefer
hilflos auf dem Ruecken lag,
seine vielen schwarzgezackten Beine
wie im Gebet zum Himmel reckte.

Ich benuetzte ein Stueck Plastik um ihn zu heben,
Ueber die Balustrade liess ich ihn in die Taxushecken fallen,
die wie Riesen Inca Koepfe geschnitten sind.

Er fiel, schwebte, flog in seine gruene Heimat.
Vaya con Dios, hermanito,
kleiner Bruder im grossen Universum.

Vaya con Dios, little brother!

Quito, Hotel Quito, Dec. 05

This morning I saved a life.
Helpless, he was lying on his back,
Useless his legs that trembled in the air,
hopeless to ever see his green ambiente, his home ever again,

Like Kafka's metamorphosed roach
he was beating, striking void air
with his many black-serrated legs.
Did he send his cry for help into the universe?

I have come to this hotel for 30 years, I never used these stairs
to go to the swimming pool.
Who or what guided me to this detour on my way to the garden,
For my daily yoga and tree energy exercise?

Did somebody—did I, hear the prayer of this humble stag beetle?
I used a piece of plastic to let him fall into the
green hedges, that are cut into huge Inca heads.
His green home.
Vaya con Dios, hermanito, little brother in the
Huge universe.

Der Narturmensch spricht zum Stadtmenschen

1988

Was weisst denn du, wie Bergwind ueber Wiesenblumen weht
der du nur Asphalt und Teer zu deinen füessen kennst

Was weisst denn du, wie Quellen Leben sprudeln
der eilig seine Autoraeder Strassenpfuetzen spritzen laesst.

Was weisst denn du, wie Lerchen jubelnd lieben
der aus Gewohnheit muede Haut der traurigen Geliebten tastet,

Was weisst denn du, wie Regen sich vermaehlt mit Erde
der Blumen nur auf Graeber pflanzt, um fuer Momente gut zu sein.

Was weisst denn du, wie Baum und Beere sich zu Wald verweben
der lieber Geld Papier, das schmutzig und bedruckt, in seinen Haenden haelt

Was weisst denn du, wie Mond und Sterne aus den Seen leuchten
der du halbblind bist vom Reklamegeschrei der Neonroehren.

Was weisst denn du, wie Liebesworte leise locken
der du halbtaub bist vom Maschinenlaerm und dem Geplaerr der Discotheken

Morgen bleibt nichts fuer deine Enkelkinder
komm mit mir und rette deine Rasse
zerstoer sie nicht mit Fetzen Zeit und Hoffnung
die auf nichts sich gruendet.

A farmer talks to a city person

1995

How do you know
How bluebells nod,
when evening breezes gently blow:
Who only knows pollution and exhaust.

How do you know
How rain and earth unite in marriage
to procreate eternal web of life:
who only knows the dirty puddles on the street
that splash all over you when cars go by.

How do you know
How moonlight plays
in your beloved's hair
Who is half blind of glaring neon lights.
Do you remember passion, laughter, lust
Who is too tired and rather watches evening news.

How do you know
how larks greet every morning full of joy,
Or, maybe, hear a nightingale at night:
Who is half deaf of blaring background noise a city makes,
the sirens, honking, and what they call music.

How do you know
How tree and berry form a tapestry of colour
Who worships dirty paper, full of empty symbols
Holding it in your hand and call it money.

How do you know
About the scent of mountain flowers
when snow is slowly melting
how they courageously expect the Spring:
who only buys flowers to put on graves
out of bad conscience or favours to obtain.

You leave nothing for posterity
Except some empty words and slogans
based on nothing
Save what is still there, plant hope and beauty, even in rags
It's better than what you do and think you have.

Maschinen

copyright 2008

Waeren wir Maschinen wuerde man uns
als untaugliches Produkt fuer immer vernichten.
Fuer jede acht Stunden Arbeit brauchen wir acht Stunden Ruhe
Um wieder volle Funktion zu erreichen.
Wir sind Treibstoff Verschwender
Der Grossteil geht unverbraucht in den Abfal Ins Klo
Und produziert unglaublich schaedliche Verunreinigung.
Wir sind gegenseitig unertraeglich unvertraeglich
Programmiert teinander zu zerstoeren.
Ein Lagerhaus voller Kisten, die einander bekaempfen
sobald der Aufseher wegschaut,waere unbrauchbar.
Programmierte Lebensdauer wird nicht erreicht,
durch faslchem Treibstoff und totaler Missachtung der Gebrauchsanweisung
Wie in den Zehn Geboten.
Nach 2 Minuten ohne Luft stirbt unser Zentral Kontroll System ab
Wir brauchen staendig neue Energie Zufuhr, vor Allen Wasser.
Luft und Wasser sind unsere primaere Lebensbedingung
Und beides zerstoeren wir ohne Bedenken.
Daher sind wir als Massenprodukt ungeeignet,
Trotzdem vermehren wir uns in geometrischer Progression
Und gefaehrden die Erde.
Vielleicht, haben einige von uns Lieberhaberwert fuer Sammler.

The machine

copyright 2008

If we were machines we soon would be discarded
As inefficient product: for every eight hours of work
We need eight hours of rest to restore full function.
We are not fuel efficient: most of the input is expelled unused,
Causing destructive pollution.
We are incompatible with each other, wired to mutual destruction.
Imagine a warehouse full of crates, battling each other
As soon as the supervisor leaves.
Expected functioning according to programmed duration
Is not reached, caused by wrong fuels
And total disregard of instructions as in the ten commandments
We cannot exist more than two minutes without air, then our main central
control dies off.
We need constant refueling, especially with water
Air and water are our main necessity and both we destroy.
Therefore we are unfit for mass production but auto-mass-produce constantly
Endangering the Earth.
Maybe some of us are valuable
To a collector of collectors' items.

Bescheidene Identitaet.

Die Mutter ist im Meer der Zeit verschwunden
so wie mein Mann, mein Freund, mein Land, ich selbst.
was hier an fernen, fremden Ufern aufgefunden
traegt meinen Namen, mein Gesicht,
doch meine Sprache spricht es nicht.

Mein Kind ist weg, verheiratet mit einem Fremden, in einem fremden Land
mit fremden Pass, ist es mir fremd.
Ich bin erstaunt, wenn jemand aus der frueheren Zeit mich trifft,
erkennt, und mich sogar beim Namen nennt.
Jedoch: Solange in der Sonne ich noch Schatten werfe,
ein Spiegel meinen Umriss reflektiert, so weiss ich,
dass mein Ich noch existiert.

Modest identity.

My mother sank into the ocean of time
so did my friends, my country
and I.
What walks
with my name
and my face
is not
I.
I am surprised
when somebody greets me on the street
does that mean
one can recognize
Me?

My child has gone
to a far, strange land
married a stranger
talks a strange tongue
is estranged
from me.

But:
as long as I throw
a shadow in the Sun
and in a mirror
I see a reflection
of my face
I know,
somewhere
there is still
a little
I.

C'est si triste avec toi…

C'est si triste avec toi
Parce que je ne peux plus te donner plaisir
Je suis triste avec toi
Parce que je te rend malheureuse.

C'est ne pas ta faute, ni la mienne
Mon petit choux
Parce que l'amour c'est comme un homme
Il vient ou il s'en va pour toujours.

C'est triste mais c'est vrai
Je sans, mon petit choux
Il n'y a plus rien entre nous,
Sauf l'adieu, l'adieu pour toujours.

Demain tu seras triste,
sans mon amour
Qui te chauffe, quit te gate,
qui te donne, qui te soin.

Tu es comme Don Juan qui a besoin
une nouvelle amour chaque jour.
Mais le bonheur ni lui, ni toi,
tu trouvera jamais.

Est que je peux venir dans ton lit
Je me ferai toute petite
pour la derniere fois je veux me sentir femme dans tes bras
peut-etre, je l'espere, la flamme se revivra.

Poem in 3 languages, none of them mine,
a la Dorothy Parker

Beware, young friends
of "les petits coques pretencieux
et dona ferentes"

Pour une femme c'est mieux
de se faire aimer
que d'aimer trop

Trop de larmes
which only harm
your skin, your heart,
your Ego.

Truemmer

Wir zertruemmern Atome
und zertruemmern die Welt
und kuemmern uns nicht
obs den Truemmern gefaellt.

Wir zertruemmern Familien
und zertruemmern den Stolz
und zertruemmern die Blumen
und zertruemmern das Holz.

Und wenn alles in Truemmern
ertoent das Geschrei
was haben wir getan?
und beginnt alles Neu.

Atomizer

We atomize atoms
and atomize joy
we don't even question
what we destroy.

We fly to the moon
and fly faster than sound
but… who walks the trail
which is—near you—around.

We fly to the moon
and fly to the stars
but—if you look up at night
they are obscured by neon light

We watch the Olympics
we watch death and crime
but—when have you watched a rosebud
or written a rhyme?

Herzenswunsch

Zurich, Oktober 09

Ich moechte einen neuen Mann, einen freien Mann, einen treuen Mann.
Er kann jung oder alt sein, soll von guter Gestalt sein, und vor allem, ohne
    Gewalt sein.
Er muss potent sein, eloquent sein, und zuhoer-persistent sein.
Er sollte ehrlich sein, sexbegehrlich sein und seelisch unversehrlich sein.
Er muss international sein, multilingual professional sein, sein Wissen
    muss kolossal sein.
Er darf mich nie kritisieren, antagonisieren, soll mich nur adorieren.
Und sehr rasch lokalisieren.

I want a new man

I want a new man, a true man a macho man.
He can be young or old,
Should have a heart of, and the pockets full, of gold
He should love lust, love and what I write,
When I need him he should never be out of sight
But when I need my space he should have the flair
To just disappear into thin air
He should admire and adore me
He must be generous, witty and kind
But most important, very soon find me.

Laerm und Stille

Morgenstau in der Iben Gavirol, Tel Aviv
Autos kriechen, hupen, fluchen
Als ob mehr Laerm
Das Rotlicht beschleunigen koennte.

Radfahrer schlaengeln sich zwischen den Wagen
Klingeln uns pfeifen und rufen "Passt auf"
Eine Harley-Davidson
Braust frech ueber den Gehsteig.

Eine geborstene Roehre ueberschwemmt
Die Strasse mit kostbarem Wasser
Die Feuerwehr bahnt sich den Weg
Mit grossem Getoese frei.

Strassenbohrer zerreissen mit teuflischem Feuer
das Pflaster
Hilflose Menschen veruschen vergeblich
die Strasse zu kreuzen

Chauffeure und Fussgaenger beschimpfen einander
Wie nur Erzfeinde es tun.
Polizisten erscheinen auf toesenden Motorraedern
Sie bruellen Befehle und vergroessern das Chaos.

Es ist zehn Uhr morgens
Der Gedenktag der Holocaust opfer
Und ihre jaehrliche
Posthume Ehrung.

Sounds and Silence

in Skidmore 07

Main Street Tel Aviv

Morning rush hour in Tel Aviv
Cars crawl bumper to bumper
Honking and cursing as if
Additional noise could speed up the lazy red light.

Bicycles wind their ways between cars
Ringing and whistling and shouting "watch out"
While a roaring Harley Davidson just uses
The sidewalk to pass.

The slow traffic is caused by a broken pipe
Allowing precious water to rush out
And flood the road as far as you can see.
Emergency sirens blow their way free
To pass.

Jackhammers start to rip into the road
With devilish force.
People helplessly try to pass or cross over.
Drivers and pedestrians cursing each other
As arch enemies do.

Police on motorbikes try to make order
They shout orders and only increase
The already chaotic mess.

Eine Bombenangriff Alarm Sirene ertoent
Alles und jeder erstarrt
Egal wo er steht,
Egal was er tut.

Die Fahrer verlassen ihr Auto
Die Tueren bleiben offen
Die Radfahrer halten ihr Rad
Die Ppolizisten ihr Motorrad.

Fuer zwei Minuten erstarrt die Stadt
in toedlicher Stille
Nur die Sirenen heulen und kreischen
Wie die Stimmen der Toten

Ihr verzweifeltes Schreien, in Panik
Ueber das Verschwinden der Lieben, des Lebens,
Das Stoehnen der gemarterten
Verhungerten Koerper und Seelen.

Die Sirenen verstummen
Der Albtraum verbleicht
Der Laerm, das Hupen und Fluchen
Das Klingeln und Droehnen und Bohren

Werden zur himmlischen Musik
Normalen Lebens, gesunder Routine
Geschuetzt durch unsere
Starke Armee.

It is 10 a.m. on Remembrance Day
When Holocaust victims,
And a week later the fallen soldiers
are honored.

A bomb alert horn blares
Everything and everybody freezes
Wherever he is, or she does.

Drivers get out of their car
Leaving the door ajar
Bicycle riders stand next to their bike
Cops hold their motorbikes.

For two long minutes deadly stillness
Reigns in the city
Except for the bomb alert horn.

Now only the dead are heard:
Their desperate cries
The shrieking pain
The panic of loss
The howling of tortured
Bodies and souls.

The horn simmers down
the nightmare fades out
the noise of the city resumes
the roaring and droning
the honking and cursing
even the jackhammer
are the heavenly music
of normal life and routine.

Emotions

Hioba

Juni 97

Oh God, should I praise you or damn you
for betting again with Satan
how much can we load on this woman
how many times more
lure her and taunt her and break her heart
and that of tiny Michelle.

Or should I thank you for walking and seeing and hearing
although the pleasure of lilacs and roses
you took away a long time ago.
Should I thank you for knees that still bend
enabling a bath in the tub without help
for walking and seeing the lake and its swans
and the walls of flowering rhododendrons
remembering when I taught the splendor of colors
to tiny Michelle

Or should I hate you, oh Lord
for showing me families, grandmothers wiping the noses of
their tiny, whatever their name
for breaking my heart with physical pain
gripping with claws of loss and despair
when my heart wants to love
and there is no one but strangers.

Or should I laud you, oh Lord
that there are strangers and friends
to fill
the abyss of loss.

Or should I leave you, Oh Lord
an illusion, a product of archaic, archetypical hopes
dreams the collective subconscious invents,
invented to strengthen the weak and the poor.
No, not strengthen
to blind and to fool them with promises that may,
or may not, be kept.
The probability, like the weather report
being fifty-fifty, however coincidence rolls.

Or should I pledge you adherence
as I did in 1942
when you saved me from Auschwitz
gave me all that I craved for
a full life, lots of love, money, success
and seeing the wonders of nature and countries
you had created
maybe just for me.

Or should I despair, as you dealt me
the three A's I dreaded the most in this world,
poor old and alone,
arm, alt und allein.

Or praise you, oh Lord, that my fingers still write
and words arise flowing as I talk to you,
realising
you are and I am and we both are the same
I am but a tiny cell, which could turn malignant
still part of the universe
that is you.
And no part or particle is ever alone.

Or, should I just ignore you, oh Lord
the worst punishment for you…

June 6th 2004, Michelle's 13th birthday

Today we lost Michelle, the court ended Marion's parental rights and the fat, ugly goia stepmother got the right to adopt her.

Ghazal for Michelle

The last time you were legally mine
You were ten and I kissed you and hugged you
 close to my heart

Then came the years of tyranny of supervisors
Of limited visits and endangered time of holding you
 close to my heart

The judge was corrupt, all visits suspended
A fortune spent on attorneys, just for the right to hold you
 close to my heart

Through conflict of interest, perjuries, lies
My opponent, your father, won and terminated my right to hold you
 close to my heart

More lawyers, appeals, and counter appeals
Many months and tears later I totally lost the right to hold you
 close to my heart

I saw you again under risk of jail
When you had your Bat Mitzvah you still were so
 close to my heart

As we could not speak, you gave me a message
That you will carry out my grandmother's goal, which always is
 close to my heart

In the most clever way: singing "Ha Tikvah"
To live as free people in our own land which always is
 close to my heart

You told me you will come there when you are eighteen
And may decide for yourself what is
    close to your heart

Only one more year I have to survive and hope and pray
That you make the right choice,
So I can kiss you and hug you and hold you

Close to my heart

In Kurt's memory

To spare me the indignity
To have to fight for his rights,
to protect my integrity
Kurt extended his lifelong, expected,
accepted, and often abused,
seldom rewarded, or reciprocated, generosity
with the ultimate and final sacrifice:

he complies and dies.

To end his solitary confinement
that was not alleviated by the gentle touch of familiar hands,
except the nurses' and mine,
the quietness not made tolerable
by the sweet sound of whispered words,
the absence of daughters and grandchildren noticed by all.
But he refused, when I wanted to call them:
"I do not want to be a burden to anybody," he wrote.
"I have nothing to give anymore," he spelled.
"I cannot survive alone," he cried…
Phonecalls, that often did not reach him, do not replace the physical
    presence providing warmth and strength.

He, who always was present, often sacrificing his own interests,
when Ann or Lili gave birth,
In Nuernberg he neglected his game career, when Lili divorced the first
    time,
In the beginning of our own life together, he first catered to his mother,
    then to engagements,
weddings, buying cars, renting apartments,
financing, organizing, setting up funds and college funds,

then there were 6 grandchildren born, there were bat and bar mitzvahs,
     with generous gifts
there were 8 birthdays every year,
and as long as there were sons in law, there were ten. Or 11 with Van. Or
     12 including Michelle or 14 with Marion and me.
And what did he get, for his last birthday, one day before we left for
     Florida? His last birthday!
One pair of heavy winter gloves.
Where are they now, all those who expected and received,
were fed innumerable lunches and dinners.
I am alone, with the mask and gloves required,
in the quietness of isolation.
For hours I squeeze my lover's hand, I whisper words of courage and
     strength,
recite places and songs of happiness,
and happy we were,
whenever, wherever,
we were alone
without phone.
I bring gifts to the nurses, and drive 3 times a day, 12 miles each time,
and never resenting it, doing what I still can,
for my last true, big love, my soul mate, my lover, my friend.
I hurt to see how Kurt, generous, sweet, always giving Kurtito,
gets nothing in return, when he needs it most.

*Written the morning, 5-6 a.m. April 12th, in the isolation hospital room,
when I realized, that we do not fly to NY this day, and never will. Kurt
died in the afternoon.*

The Credo of a Pioneer of the Longevity Species

I claim the right to age with grace
Without apologies that I am still alive.
That I still breathe air and use my assets
That my heirs crave.

I prefer to wear my face with wrinkles
Rather than a Botox mask screwed on an old body.
A friendly smile seems more attractive
than a porcelain forehead without a trace of thoughts.

I claim the right to sit and read without bad conscience
Although the Gym is waiting with weights and steps.
In the park I prefer to walk, to look, to talk, to think
Instead of jogging.

I enjoy my meals because my body is healthy;
I do not have to be size 8 anymore.
My cholesterol is high but my blood pressure is low,
And both are steady.

I claim the right to sleep or wake according to my rhythm,
Not rules of an old age home, however fancy their euphemisms are.
I claim the right to bathe or shower as often as I like,
To eat or not to eat, to take the pills or throw them in the garbage.

To walk or sit, to write or think. To phone or watch TV—
All of the above you take for granted.
All of the above are my undisputed rights,
As long as I am independent.

I claim the right to drive my car,
As I can see far;
My reactions are fast,
My experience vast.

I claim these rights and pray to God
To protect them, to live free, not under the control
Of young unskilled help, who, subconsciously
Or in the open, are hostile.

In homes created to produce profit, disregarding human dignity.
I claim the right to believe in Dr. Choprah and the Bible—
Both promise us one hundred and twenty years of healthy life,
Based on the length of our pregnancy.

Therefore I need projects, love, friends and laughter
To fill them and to wish and want to claim my eternal,
Uncurtailed, indestructible, unadulterated,
Unequivocal, undiminished, unmistakably inviolable, inalienable,
Immutable, incorruptible, irretrievable, irrefutable RIGHTS.

Macao

The story of Macao in 20 seconds: It was Chinese, for 400 years it was Portugese, now it is Chinese again, a gambling island. The owner of the casino of my poem collects jade sculptures, in white or green—even lavender and pink—weighing many tons, 3-4 yards high, intricately carved, behind glass cages.

The poem is to read very rhythmically, like the clicking of the stacks of chips.

—February 2002

I never knew his name
But I remember the frame
Of the man in the game.
One bodyguard at left and
One bodyguard at right
He sat in the middle
In the blinding stark light.

Right hand on the stack
Left hand moves to bid
no cigar on his lip
But it looks as if he did.

Between his hands
a stack of chips
He shoves the stack
on the betting line
He opens two cards,
He has a six and a nine.

The girl in wine
Who holds the banc
Opens two cards
She has a seven and a nine.

The man with no name
And no cigar between his lips
Has just lost a million
But he continues the game.

The bodyguard behind his back
Hands him another high stack
his Chinese face shows no emotion
his Chinese hand bets the high stack.

No cigar and no name
No conscience and no shame
All around the table lost
But he does not care.

His Chinese face is
Like a terracotta mask
It does not move
Neither do his guards.

The stack of chips
Looks like a scepter in his hand
He demonstrates he is the master
Over this Portugese land.

The bodyguard who guards his back
Hands him another double stack
Neither cigar, nor name, nor shame
He is still in the game

The same evening, much later
I met him in the elevator.
One bodyguard at left and one bodyguard at right
Now he had a cigar between his lips
The three just walked over me
As if I were… not there.

Corrida—Mi lindo Quito

Plaza de toros, fiestas 2002

Noon sharp—the hymn fills the sky
"Gloria a ti, patria mi…"
We sing under the glaring sun,
And I have no hat
To press against my breast
As 15,000 aficionades do, singing
"mi pecho rebozo."
The ticket says shade, but there is no shade
on the equator at noon.
The only loge with a roof is reserved
For the president of this show
And his vassals.

The gates fly open.
The priests solemnly approach
across the width of the round:
Two in medieval garb
two on heavily padded horses, pikes exposed.
　　Four and four in costumes, decorative but modest
　　to give all the light to the three stars
　　who today will perform
　　the dance of love and death
　　in their traje de luces
　　heavily embroidered in gold
　　to attract and protect by reflecting the rays of the sun,
　　and expose the most vital parts of their gracious bodies
　　from the waist down.

Here speaks the bull:
If you could choose, would you rather
Be hauled to a slaughterhouse, after a short existence,
confined, fed hormones and chemicals,
without sun, without space to move
to precipitously increase the weight of your flesh.
Squeezed in trucks without air,
Hearing the pain and smelling the blood of your peers,
until it is your turn to be forced to the machine
that will kill you without pardon—without grace.

    Or—speaks the bull:
I lived like a prince for four or five years,
pampered, fed only the best,
roaming freely on pastures and fields.
I got strong and graceful,
my pelt a shining armour in black.
I ran with my peers,
humans attended to my every need.

Then, at one special noon, the gates fly wide open
I enter, I am greeted by music
and humans in colorful garb,
Waving mantillas in red, pink or blue,
an invitation to play.
They disappear, leave the field to a splendorous man,
The one I saw eye to eye a few days ago.
His presence is full of light, blinding my eyes.

I stand still to admire my playmate, my love.
He approaches—stops—stands,
shows me his breasts and the parts
that prove he is a man, equal to me.

Tenderly his soft voice calls:
"Toro-torito,"
the name I always was called.
His voice is soft and luring
I step towards him, he steps towards me
Our eyes lock for eternity.
I greet him, lowering my head to acknowledge his presence,
I show my joy by pawing the sand…
He suddenly turns, leaving me sad and abandoned—
Did I offend this glamorous man?
He walks away as if I did not exist.

Two figures on horses ride in the round,
I feel anger and wrath as these monsters have driven away
My friend… my love.
Wild with wrath, I attack one, I hardly feel the stab,
Just the warmth of my blood, wetting my pelt.
I lift the heavy horse, it falls to its side.
Here are the first playmates again and I follow them
expecting to play, but they run away
and hide behind the wooden wall.
My anger grows and
I want to return to my fields.
Along the wall of wood I trot
To find the door,
But there is no door, no exit, no way back.
Now I feel pain, as unknown enemies
stick sticks in my back and disappear.
I am alone in the width of sun and sand
Bleeding, desperate,
As I hear his voice again,
So soft, sweet, loving, luring:
"Toro, torito."
I run towards him, we dance the dance of love:
He kneels before me, he strokes my horns, he strokes my bleeding back,
I do not feel pain, I do not feel my blood, just joy,
As we turn and move around each other's bodies.

All those humans in festive attire
watch and join our fun
With music and clapping their hands
And shouting "ole."

Our dance grows faster and wilder,
Again he kneels in front of my eyes.
I won't hurt you, my friend, you trust me, exposing
Your most vulnerable protruding parts,
exuding your manhood.

He rises, he turns—walks away, again, abandoning me.
I feel pain, I am tired, alone in the sun.
Where is the door to go home?
There he returns, soft, sweet, loving, luring
"Toro torito!"
I run towards him: Where is the mantilla we played with before?
He is hiding something in the red rag
Which he waves before my head.
I squint my eyes to catch his eyes,
To understand what he means?
Now I understand: we dance the dance, not of love
but of death.
My epiphany:
my destiny is to die for your glory!
Willingly I follow your lead.
Again I dance with you,
for you to display your body, your courage, your grace.
I die for you, my playmate, my lover, my god,
Just grant me one more glance of the splendour
Of your victory in the sun.
Our eyes lock as I fall,
Your hands wave in front of my eyes
The eternal good bye.
I die: A martyr of love.

Stierampf: Hier Spricht der Stier

Quito—Ecuador—12 Uhr mittag.
Die Hymne erklingt, 15.000 Menschen pressen ihre Huete an die Brust,
meistens Panama huete und singen voll Andacht und Inbrunst…
Gloria a ti, Patria—il pecho rebozo…
Ich habe teuere Tickets im Schatten gekauft—
mittags am Aequator ist kein Schatten,
die einzigen Sitze unter einem Daechlein sind
fuer den Praesidenten dieser show
und seine Vasallen reserviert.

Die Priester treten ein—streng nach Kasten geordnet—
Der Oberpriester in glitzerndem Ornat, der Matador, der Toeter
Der Picador zu Pferd

Hier spricht der Stier:

Als meine Zeit, geboren zu werden, gekommen war,
hatte ich die Wahl ein kurzes, stures, dumpfes Leben zu fuehren,
vielleicht ein Jahr, gedraengt in engem Stall,
gefuettert mit Hormonen und Antiobiotics.

Nie frei, nie in der Sonne, nie mit meinesgleichen laufen und spielen.
Hoechst wahrscheinlich kastriert. Das Ende ist qualvoll
in Lastwagen eingepfercht, ohne Luft,
voll Angst und Verzweiflung.
Manchmal versucht einer auszubrechen, er wird in den engen Gang gezwaengt,
mit eisernem Hammer zrrtruemmern sie den Schaedel meiner Artgenossen
—ihr Blut steigt mir in die Nase—keine Ausweg—keine Luft—
    keine Hoffnung,
nur das elende Geschrei rund um mich,
das Ende, wie mein ganzes Leben,

eine einzige Qual. Der Tod kommt als Erloesung.

Oder die Alternative:
4 oder 5 Jahre lebe ich wie ein Prinz, gehegt und gepflegt,
frische Wiesen bieten mir das beste Futter,
mit meiner Herde spiele ich, laufe mit der Sonne um die Wette,
manchmal auch raufen wir, bis ich stark werde.
die Muskeln wie gehaemmert, mein Fell ein schwarz
    schimmernder Panzer…

Ich bin (werde) zum Kaempfen geboren und erzogen—
und wenn ich mich nicht besiegen lasse,
wenn ich den Kampf gewinne,
wird mein Samen kostbar wie Gold.
ich werde die erlesensten Partnerinnen begatten,
gehegt wie ein Koenig, meine einzige Funktion ist
viele neue edle Kampfstiere in die Welt zu setzen,
mein Name beruehmt und meine Zuechter bereichert.

Und jetzt ist er da, "der Augenblick der Wahrheit:"
Das Tor fliegt auf, ich werde von Musik empfangen,
von vielen tausend Stimmen begruesst,
eine Musikkapelle spielt,
das ganze Rund voll Menschen steht und singt zu meinen Ehren.

Ich geniesse es im Mittelpunkt der Bewunderung zu stehen—
Die Sonne steht genau ueber mir—
ich werfe keinen Schatten.
ein wunderbar geschmueckter Mensch erscheint,
in ploetzlichem Erkennen treffen sich unserer Augen,
Erkennen einander, als ob wir uns schon ewig kannten.

Eine Welle von Liebe fuer diesen Mann erfuellt mich.
Ich tanze mit ihm, nach streng geregeltem Ritual
Den Tanz von Liebe und Tod.

Zaertlich umkreist, umschmeichelt er mich,
raunt Liebesworte in meine Hoerner,
Toro, torito, Stierchen komm her

So lockt er mich seinen Regeln zu folgen
Unsere Fahne schwingt nach rechts oder links
Ich tue was immer er will.

Ich fuehle nicht die Stiche der Diener
Ich sehe nur ihn, den Helden, den Gott
Zu dessen Ehren ich geopfert werde,

ich mich opfern lasse
mit Blumen und Musik
Und ich sterbe voll Liebe
In den Armen des Helden
Die Menschen rufen voll Inbrunst
Anstatt Amen—
Ole!

Longevity is a lonely land.

Tel Aviv 25.3.2011

There was a time I had a child in school,
a husband working in the Dan Hotel
With all the privileges of the chain.
A daily, loyal, full time Oseret (maid)
And a handful of discreet lovers.

I had parents, a brother,
and made a lot of money in the market.
A chevrah (group) of elegant, beautiful women and successful men,
All couples, with interchangeable partners.

A big party every Friday evening,
A picnic every Shabbat in the unspoiled forests,
on the way we visited the chimpanzee family
with the egoistic male.

My husband and I had to get away,
He from this despotic, possessive mother,
I from my spoiled child.
We had a day away, every week,
in one of the chain's luxurious resorts.

Parents, brother, all three husbands went
where everybody ends,
As did friends and lovers.
Those still around are in homes, or homebound,
Cannot walk, cannot do anything but moan.

There on the beach sits a lonely lady,
Dreaming, writing about the time that was good
And she did not know it.

Maybe that goes for now too:
I am still free to come and go,
to walk, to eat, to use my money.
So what if I do it alone:
Enjoy the day! carpe diem!
and do not groan!

I am not Dylan Thomas

10.Dec.2011

I will not go gentle into that good night,
Not for a long time to come
And if, or rather, when I go
I go with rage and roar
Directly from this good light
Into hopefully a better light.
Whether wise, or good or brave
Or just a man, and in my case a woman,
We never know what we leave behind,
Which word triggered a better word,
Which glimmer of ideas would stimulate
Somebody, you might not even know
To improve, invent, create a better world.

I shall not go gently,
As it is easier to die
In battle, in a noble fight
For every bit of the last light.

Goethe's last words were: "plus lucis"—Mehr Licht!

Sisyphus remembered.

Fall 2003

Is this a penitentiary that never has heard of human rights,
Or a corner in hell, punishing sinners with torture?
Wherever I look I see twisted bodies, heaving, groaning, moaning,
Running and running and arriving nowhere.
They lift weights that fall down, to be lifted again the next moment,
Getting heavier with every lift
And there, bending sideways, up and down, an old woman, her hair,
white as snow, forming a tiny curtain
hiding her face.
Up and down she bends witout end.
Another old woman lies on her back, her knees at angle to push or pull
an invisible load.
And there—stairs to be climbed to eternity,
without gaining height,
One next to the other—three, four,
climbing stairs, staring ahead into the void.
They climb and climb,
They run and run,
They bend and bend and lift and lift
And pay for it dearly
in the fitness club—"to build better bodies."
And I am one of them.

This morning I changed this routine
I danced with Elmo, from Channel thirteen,
the happy-happy dance and the hokey-pokey,
I stepped like Fred Astaire, with the Sesame Street kids.
What a difference a channel makes:
music and fun instead of violence and guns.

I stepped onto my porch
and for the first time I took the time to notice
The outburst of my hydrangea,
White waves turning to faint pink and bronze.
Instead of rushing to the gym
The last bite of breakfast dripping into the grass,
Hopping into the car, not stopping at any light,
Hurrying, scurrying to the Gym,
I saluted the sun from my deck.
I breathed and stretched with the cat,
Without the noisy hip-hop beat and rap
And the ruthless commands of the coach.
But, actually, instead of getting my heartbeat up and my weight down
I sit and I write, and what does that do for my joints?

I am

Nov. 3 03

I am the kiss I did not kiss
And the book I did not write
I am my husband whom I miss
And I am the eagle in flight.

I am the earth around the Sun
And the Sun around the earth
I am here, and I am fun
I am the cradle, I am the hearse.

If I have to cry…

Swan Lake, Summer 2004

If you have to cry
Cry into the fur of a cat
(Or any other furry small pet.)

If I do—I feel her little heart beat
In the same rhythm as mine.
Her warm body replaces
the other body which comforted me
When I had a hard time.

Her purring reminds me that affection,
Love Trust and Hope are still there,
My smile takes the place of the last tear
Because I know:

my time is not up
If somebody still needs me,
even if it is only a cat with her soft purr
and my tears in her fur.

I learned from her to stretch and to breathe,
To salute the sun and do as I please
Any command I refuse to obey
As the cat does: when I call her, she looks away.
I learned to ignore machine messages galore
Like e-mails and faxes and bills more and more,

I am generous and share a dollar and a dime
My clothes, umbrellas and even a rhyme
The only things I am stingy with
Is my cat and my time.

The hedonist

My brain stores the lights
of sunsets and dawns
of flowers that nod to the nights.
It stores many jokes
told my friend on my lawn
it knows music and paintings
and landscapes and sights.

A full-blooded Hedonist
looking for joy
not very useful to mankind
am I.

But I do not destroy
young people with drugs
nor do I produce guns for war.
I do not sell components
for bombs to kill or scar
I do not ship weapons to Poland.

What is preferable
to passively enjoy
or actively destroy?

   —sincerely yours, hedonist

What I am a genius of

I am a meddlesome old lady
Who shares her wisdom with anybody who does not want to hear it.

I am called Dr. Inge, although I am not a doctor
I still dispense advice and the matching pills to take.

I interrupt total stranger' conversations
And answer questions that are not addressed to me.

I speak my mind on politics and war
But not about the stock exchange, of which I really am an expert.

I speak about all my past and present lovers
Except the one that really counted.

Beware of my advice, it might be wrong all over,
And flee if you can, from this kind of kind old ladies.

Feast of life

I am included in the feast of life
I am the life
I am the feast
I am a tiny cell
in the creator's universal body
I am important to the balance of it all.
If I am cancerous
I might begin the end.
We are one
I can itch the system
I can destroy it,
the almighty creator
may, or may not
be aware of me.
But we are one

I am included in…
I am the feast of life.

Tavern on the Green

9/25/02

Rekindling the love of yesteryear
Seems funny first, nostalgic,
Zaertlich.
Repeating romance,
by dancing in the moonlight
big band is playing in
Tavern on the Green
The music of our youth

Grateful to God:
Not only am I—
are we—here,
But everything functions
From knee to brain.
Going home,
"as if,"
As if we had been married
For these fifty elapsed years
Warm, no stress, no tension,
Just a lot of laughter, not about us,
But about all the others,
Most of them gone.

The night,
new, no repetition, no plagiarism,
It's all new, a new beginning.

God, I am grateful
Not only am I—are we—what a wonderful word,
"We"
Here,
And everything functions.

Hungry in Hua-Hin

1993

I am hungry for a hungry mouth
to hurt my lips
when unwilted passion passes
from thigh to thigh
furrowing deep in space and time to evoke the spark of life once more
or again
or maybe.
ivory lithe limbs
bulging lumps of muscles
promising, tempting
tasting of youth

Raetsel

Ich bin winzig doch stark
Allein im Meer der Vereinigung
Geheimnis ist Gesetz
Reichtum ist geheim
Ich bin arm doch reich durch Arbeit.
Wenn meines gleichen fallen
Steige ich in Wert.
Niemand liebt mich
Doch will sein wie ich
Die Loesung sind drei Worte
Jedes fuer sich
Doch alle drei eine Einheit

Loesung
Schweiz, Bankgeheimnis—Schweizer Franken Waehrung

Poems by Inge Ginsberg in Carol's class

The riddle
I am tiny but strong among my peers
Isolated within an unified sea
Secrecy is law
And Wealth is secret
I am poor but rich thru work
When my peers fall, I rise (in value)
Nobody loves me but wants to be me.
The solution are three words
Each alone but all connected.

Switzerland
not member of the EU
bank secrecy is law in the Swiss constitution

The Swiss currency

Sex and Lovers

My first year as a widow

My first years as a widow I had a cat
I cried into her fur, she slept in my bed.
The second year, in Israel, I met Martin, hired him as chauffeur and cook,
He was 30 years younger, after I slept with him, I was the cook.
We lived happily in the Land of the Thai
From Hua Hin in the South, to the North, called Shang-rai
But he got involved with the Chinese Mafia in Siam
I got scared and I ran.

Next was Gilbert my big love at first night
He played me like a Stradivari,
In bed, car and table, he did everything right.
My daughter conspired with his former mistress
That bitch needed his money to my big distress
The first time in my lifetime I loved and was left.

The next day I had a blind date in a café near my flat
I had cried and was messy, just wanted to tell him
I was not ready for a new rat.
I met Jossi, good looking with his broad friendly grin
We spent six peaceful months, were in Budapest and in Berlin
Tenderness and affection had replaced uncontrollable passion.
In August Tel Aviv called him back—
and now

The absurd is in the eye of the beholder, Michael said
He is 35 years younger, a hunk and rich,
But the only friend he has is his cat.
He loves me with passion, as no man for a long time had,
Even if it is fool's paradise, I take what I get.

Ode to my married lover

Jan. 3rd 05

My married lover and I play the game
That we are lovers
in a romantic romance
That is still alive.

We play to make passionate dates,
Only to cancel them
either you or I,
Any pretext serves that purpose.

We both would miss this game
So let's continue to make
Sweet phone calls,
Mostly to machines

Sweet encounters full
of melancholy jokes.
Big plans that never
Will come to fruition

Like Spring in the Galil
Or skiing in Davos
Or a trip around the world
On the never ever cruise.

Vielleicht

NY, 12.12.13

Meine Haut hungert nach deiner Haut,
sie duerstet nach deinem Dunst, deinem Duft
dem Schweiss in deinen Achseln
wenn deine Beine mich unfangen
kann ich, vielleicht, wieder auf Berge kraxeln.
Wenn deine Arme mir Staerke schenken,
Kann ich mich, vielleicht, wieder im Meer versenken
Die Wellen beherrschen, den Wind zujubeln.
Im Schatten deines Rueckens kann ich
vielleicht
Wieder ruhig schlafen,
ohne Angst und ohne Neurosen,
Vielleicht ruhig atmen, ohne Stress,
ohne Tosen der Umwelt,
vielleicht heilt Haut die hungrige Haut
vielleicht… vielleicht…

Seventy nights of wasted skin

8/30 2008

Seventy nights of wasted skin
　　Why, just tell me why?
Why don't I see the glitter in your eye
Your fingertips searching down my spine
Where went the heat? even warmth would be fine.
Where is the passion to fill emptiness
The seventy lonely days lost,
Just to eat, sleep and maybe rhyme?
Do you remember the big bang
Connecting us to each other
And to eternal time.

Orgasmus mit Liebe

Zurich, 15.12.12

Das ist ein sich Verlieren
Und ein sich Wiederfinden
Ein sich Geben ohne Schranken
Ohne Grenzen, ohne Gedanken
Ganz weit.

Es ist ein heiliges Erbeben
Ein sich Hin-ergeben
Zum Tanz mit den Sternen
Eins zu sein ohne Raum, ohne Zeit
zu zweit.

Die Pforte des Vertrauen
Ist eine weite Oeffnung
Man klimmt, man steigt bis zur Erschoepfung
Bis zur Explosion der Ur-Schoepfung
Seit Ewigkeit.

Orgasmus ohne Liebe

Rasch hinein und rasch heraus
Hauptsache Entspannung,
Nur meine ist wichtig.
Unwichtig ist wer oder was du bist
Fuer diesen Moment bist du richtig.

Gefuehle sind vorgetaeuscht und erfunden
Denn schon in wenigen Stunden
Feiert man die naechsten Runden
Egal mit wem, Hauptsache Du bist neu
Das Herz bleibt sowieso leer und glaubt, es sei frei.

Stradivari

March 2006

Du verzauberst mich in eine Stradivari
Aus der du Toene lockst
Die nicht fuer oder von Geigen sind.
Aus dem Urwald kommen sie
Oder aus archetypal Traeumen
Primordiales Bruellen, Stoehnen
Grunzen, Groehnen.

Eine Geige ohne Bogen
Ist nur schlecht verformtes Holz
Egal ob sie steht liegt
Oder liegend traeumt
Erst ein paar Haare
von des Pferdes Schwanz
Auch das total dem Erstzweck fern entfremdet
Erst die Verflechtung von Natur und Kunst
Fantasie und Realverhalten
Schafft die Zaubertoene
Einer Stradivari.

Du dirigierst mich wie ein Symphonie Orchester
Einfuehrung zoegernd sanft
oft wie die Pastorale,
Morgenaufgang's Vogelgezwitscher
Oder sofort herrisch wild
Ein Solo 3 Satz Appassionata
Dann Ruhe, Warten, 2 Satz von Mozart's 7th
troestend, zaertlich, ohne Hast und Eile
Oder lieblich spielerisch wie

Das Forellenquintett.
Schubert's unerwartet boeses Aufwallen
Aufgestautes, hemmungslos, mitleidlos.
Immer fuehrend bis zum erloesenden Finale.
Unvollendet, nie zu vollenden, nie zu enden
Suesse Melodien, Thema mit Variationen
Lange Soli einzelner Instrumente, alle Wege
Zum gleichen Ziel: urtuemliche Explosion,
Big Bang's Lied an die Freude

The wannabe cat

I wish I were your cat
I always could sit on your lap
While I graciously allow you to scratch my back.
You serve me specials that I detest
You think that normal food I cannot digest.
To punish you I will not eat at all
To bring you to your knees, your eyes full of love and despair
I pretend to fall.
Please eat, just a little bite, you beg.
Inside myself I grin,
I really can't, I stuffed myself with the goodies
I stole from the garbage bin.
My goal is to keep your mind preoccupied
I make you drive hundreds of miles
Just to make me happy, just to see me smile
I want to be your cat—for a while.

Nachts.

Nachts trennt uns nichts.
Haut auf Haut klebt Koerper an Koerper, waermend, staerkend, schuetzend
schirmen wir einander ab
vor den Anderen,
den Kindern, den Sorgen, dem Krebs.

Nachts gehoert Dein Atem mir
heiss draengt sich dein hurtiger Koerper
wie der eines hungrigen Kindes an die Mutterbrust.
Erloesung suchend und findend.
Nachts gehoert dein Atem mir.

Nachts wacht die Angst.
Schuettelt mich im Frost des Entsetzens,
bedroht meinen Koerper
diese Antenne der Freude und des Dankes an Gott
fuer Wind und Sonne, Berg und Meer,
droht mit langsamen oder schnellem Verfaulen.

Nachts wacht deine zaertliche Hand ueber meinem Koerper
schuetzt, waermt, und vertreibt Krankheit und Angst.

Das Herz vergisst nie

Text: Inge Ginsberg

Wir tanzten im Mondschein
Wir kuessten im Wald
Dein Bett war mir Heimat
Dein Arm hielt mich warm

Das Herz vergisst nichts
Die Haut vergisst nie
Dein Kuss brennt noch heisser
Ich fuehl dich fuer immer
im Blut.

Schlag die Tuer nicht zu!

Bitte schlag die Tuer nicht zu
sie geht nicht wieder auf
und wenn etwas herunterfällt
das geht nicht wieder rauf.

Wenn etwas zerbrochen wird
das wird nie wieder ganz
und was einmal verrostet ist
kriegt nie wieder den Glanz.

Wenn du nur verbrauchst
benuetzt, missbrauchsts, verletzt
wenn du nichts wachsen laesst
und Altes nicht ersetzt,

bleibt nur zurueck was niemand will
und niemand brauchen kann.
Und ist es mal kaputt…

Think again

Delray Beach, 14.1.08

You imagine that we roll Day and night making out, making love
On the carpet, in the kitchen In the Ocean, even, occasionally,
In the bed
Think again:
Think: living chaste Not dare to touch. Crave to be touched. At least like
the cat.
Skin is so hungry for warm healing hand.
Long sleepless nights to uphold the illusion of age-defying love
With trophy boy. Think again: With catastrophy boy.
Think Onan, why God killed him
Think of sinning against love.
Does he really think we lead
A perfect, blissful life?
Maybe we do, just that hungry skin asks too much.
Vaya con Dios, my… no
think again: You can stay but I go—no—I run.
But think again: good chauffeur in his white Porsche,
Teaches me bridge and likes to walk,
Only eats oats and greens which he shops
Together whatever I want or need,
Except you know… I thought again, what grandmother taught:
too good to throw out but too bad to wear.
If only hungry skin could be fed at least like his cat.

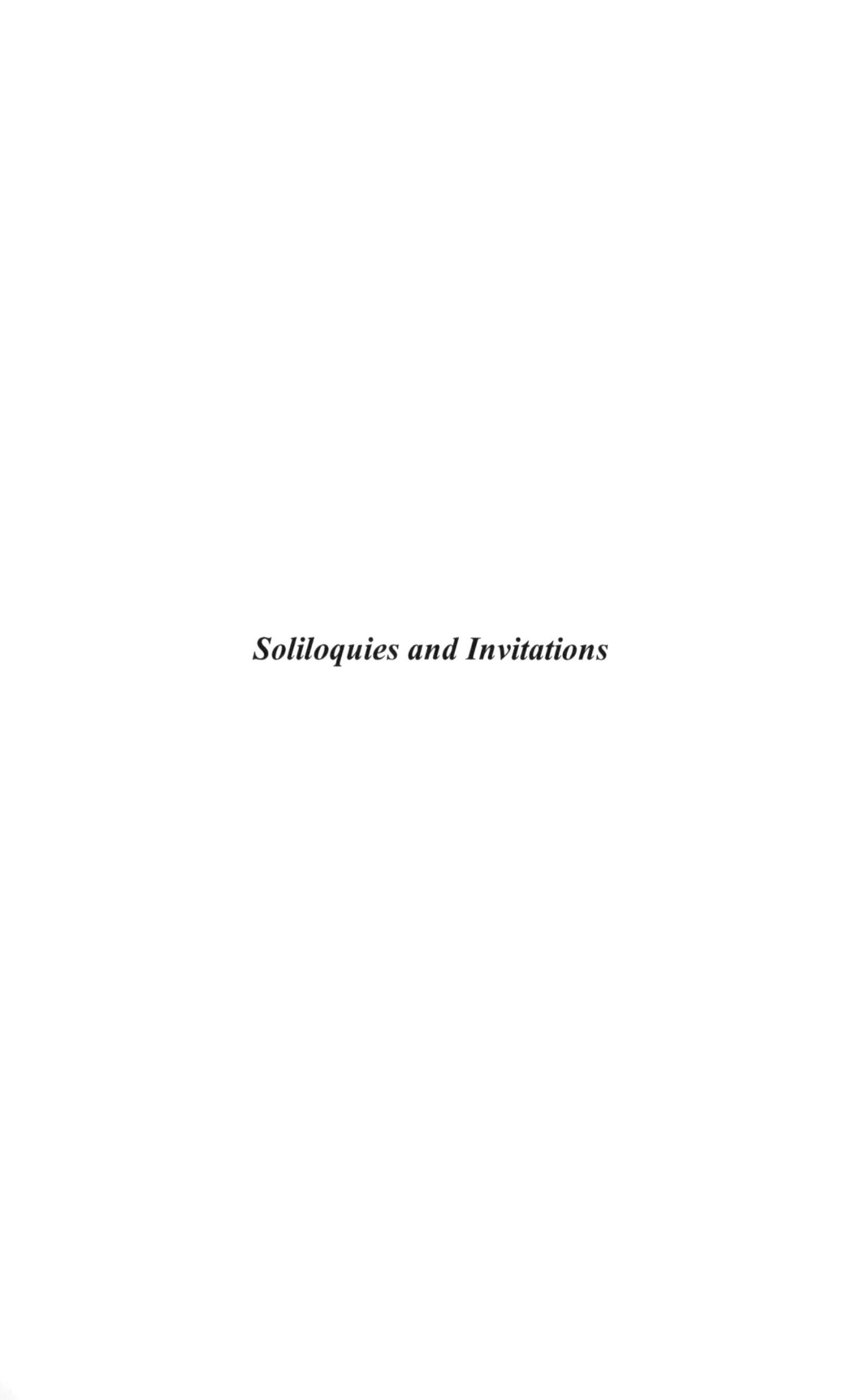

Soliloquies and Invitations

Invitation—in Tel Aviv

Zena, 1994

I heard so much about the good, hard, bad, tough time
when Zena was, instead of Caviar.
When bank accounts were small, but so were ulcers too.
When luxury it was to find a tramp
and spend a weekend in Nathania
was more than you would dare to dream.
But young you were, in spirit, soul and courage
and better clad you Zionut than Lola Baer.

So, for one night, I beg you, come as you were in 1946-8, forty six to eight,
and forget what in the meantime you put on in wealth and weight.

No Whisky and no shrimps you find tonight,
but if you find your own, forgotten self, it is worth the sacrifice
(and cheaper for me too.)

Tenue: your best of 1947

Meiner Feundin Madeleine

Zurich, 22 November 2009

Der stete Fels im Auf und Ab des Lebens
Die staemmige Eiche in deren Schatten
Man Rat und Schutz sucht und erhaelt.
Der Magnet, der unveraenderlich
Die beinahe Heimat repraesentiert
Die Inspiration zum Schlager, der,
Mit Dean Martin, es zur Hitparade schaffte,
Der Mensch, der alle Geheimnisse kennt
Und sie huetet, wie seine eigenen,
Der einen nie verriet
In genau 60 Jahren treuer Freundschaft
Die wir beide er-und ueberlebten,
Und hoffentlich bis zu 120 fortsetzen.

Fuer Janki:

Huete den heimischen Herd
verhuete,
dass heimliches Heute
dich vertreibe
von Heimat und Heim.
Liebliche, leibliche Lust lohnt
wenn Lieben und Leben
sich paaren zu lauterem Bund.
Sonst is es Schund.

The Chinese Knew
—for Doritt and Bob

16.1.99

The Chinese knew
that it takes two
to be complete. therefore please do
continue to
be the perfect two
as you did hitherto.

The vases' blue
is a symbol of being true
to your friends and to each other
just continue
as you were hitherto.

For many years
into the future,
I wish for you
to be healthy, successful and together like glue
as you are hitherto.

For Hilde

I used to write a song for you
and what I said was always true
a friend like you is hard to find
so loyal, good and sweet and kind;

many more songs I hope to sing
to your birthdays honoring
you are a woman—I repeat
loyal, kind and good and sweet.

Family and friends should all now join
to sing together this little rhyme:
Hildele till 120, in good mood
stay as you are
Sweet and kind and much too good.

Ich habe mit Gott geredet

Ich habe mit Gott geredet
und er kam
ein froehlicher junger Mann
der nichts illegales tun kann
Zum Beispiel Falschgeld machen
oder Ehebrechen.
Aber er hat Karten zu ausverkauften Stuecken,
er hat Hotelzimmer wo keine mehr sind,
er bringt Waerme und Spass und Lachen.
und dann verkauft er die story
an einen Filmagenten,
den er im ausverkauften Hotel unterbringt,
dann hatte er Geld und lachte
Mir traeumte,
ich rechtete mit Gott…

Eos, goddess of dawn

Meet my friend Eos
who colors dull grays
into the soft pink of babyfaces,
or the delicate shades of flamingos.
Still surrounded by the violets of the night,
She embroiders golden edges around ordinary forms.

Eos, my good friend, saves me from the lonely horrors of the night,
announcing Apollo, her brother, the sun.
Meet my friend Eos, goddess of the morning dawn
whose fingertips are roses
and their touch creates light.
Meet me and her
every morning before seven
at the beach…

Detox

June 2003

Sie haben das Brot mir vergiftet,
Mich geaergert gruen und blass
Die einen mit ihrer Liebe,
die andern mit ihrem Hass
—Heine

Dr. Choprah teaches me how to live to 120.
In good health
James Redfield—"celestine prophecies" teaches
"protect your energy."

It is easy to detox your body
It is easy to detox your room,
But how do you detox your liver
So full of anger and gloom.

Like thieves in the night they steal
Your energy, strength and joy,
Detox your life of the moaners
Those who always complain and cry.

And those who intimidate and question
Whatever you do or are
or those who are "aloof"
Avoid them like cholera.

Avoid those who make you feel guilty
Of guilt that you never knew
Avoid the "poor me's" which will suck
Your life's energy out of you.

Forget those, you think, who harmed you
Aeons ago in another life
Just greet them if you meet them
And forget any past strife.

Avoid the groaners and moaners,
Who hate the sun, the rain and the sky
Who never like a movie,
a concert, a show or a play.

Avoid the criers and sighers
Who report in detail their pains
What the doctor told them. And why
Is to relate a death their biggest joy?

Surround yourself, like Caesar
With friends who like sex, sleep and food
Who live, love work and feel
What happens, in the end is good.
                    (gam se le tovah)
Sip Joy from a flower
And strength from a tree
The monk in Shangmei taught me:
Just sit and just be.

    (when I came running and said "I only have ten minutes today,"
    he asked me, "how do you know that? Maybe you have only one.")

Humor

Mink

Nov. 2004

To the melody: "If you're happy and you know it clap your hands"

We're 3 girls in sheared mink that look like fake
we're 3 girls in sheared mink that look like fake
one is green and one is brown
and the black is new in town
we're 3 girls in sheared mink that look like fake.

We go out each night and paint the town in pink
we go out each night and paint the town in pink
we go out each night in mink
and we paint the town in pink
we are happy and we show it in our mink.

We're going out each night to town
und wir sind herrlich anzuschaun
wir sind herrlich anzuschaun,
because we're dressed in black and green and brown
when we are going out each night to town.

Because we are happy in our mink let's sing
let's sing about our mink, please let's sing
they might look as if they're fake,
but they are real, for God's sake,
let's now sing about our mink, let's sing.

To my friends and entertainment managers
Sabina and Rita
With love

Freedom of Affluence

September 20

I went to the city to attend to the chores of the rich.
broker, two banks, safe, shopping and manicure.
I packed all the necessary tools
for above activities into my purse

and forgot the purse in my country house
when in a hurry I left.
The friend who drove me had twenty-three dollars
In his pocket, he gave me twenty.

With which I did what all poor people do
when they get into unexpected money:
I went to gorge myself in the nearest restaurant
"Le pain quotidien" is the Christian prayer:

"Give us our daily bread," which we all take for granted.
For the first time I had to order, not what I wanted,
But what is cheaper than the twenty dollars I had.
I ordered my favorite tartine, but could not afford coffee or salad.

I never eat salad, I detest that rabbit food
Now that I could not afford it, I craved it like Robin Hood
the money of the rich.
Next to me sat a nice young woman, reading,

and absentmindedly fingering her greens.
I must get her salad, so I started a literary conversation,
Then offered her a slice of my tartine against some of her salad.
Smiling she refused the sandwich and pushed

her whole plate of greens towards me,
I am full, she said and left and I devoured that whole plate.
Maybe the rabbits are not as dumb as they look.
The tartine went home with me in a box.

Now what? for the banks I had no I.D.
for the safe I had no key.
For the broker I had no idea what I wanted to discuss
For shopping no money and no credit card.

I had nothing, but I had time!
Free as a bird or rather like a fish
I went to my club and swam without stress.
I had time for small talk and to look

At the view from my 45th floor
Over the roofs of Manhattan
Where the rich people run
in their invisible hamster wheel.

Love Brings AIDS

Gray Rock, 8. Juni 1985

Love brings AIDS
woods bring Lyme
Fruit brings poison
parking a fine.

Breathe pollution
food kills your heart
there is deadly danger
if you take a walk in the park.

forgive us, poor kids,
Freedom is your illusion
we had forty good years
we leave you an ugly world.

The ideal guest

"Oh no no no no no nooooo, I would never do that!!!"

Whatever I offered her as good hosts do—
she had it better at home, bigger, newer,
a more intricate model:
Her toaster oven rings and her microwave sings.
And if she did not have it,
her sister does, the sister that reached
the uppermost level of the social pyramid
and is admired, probably envied,
quoted almost every moment.
And if neither she nor her sister owns or does better,
So her mother's second cousin used to have or did it,
Or even the uncle, who once lived in Leeds, the one who had a butler,
Well, not really a butler,
a man who chauffeured and gardened.

"I bought this ring in Alaska," I said
I try to overtrump her bragging—"in the almost unreachable store,
North of Fairbanks, behind it are no roads, just small planes—"…
"Oh, of course, my sister took that trip, not to Fairbanks though, she
      would not dream to
leave the luxury ship."

"Last year in Shangmei I learned from a monk just to sit and do nothing…
Just be."
"For this you have to go so far? Where is this Shangmei," she asks.
"In Thailand."
"Oh, Thailand, of course, we were there, but we just stayed one night in
      Bangkok, that
was enough.

But my cousin was there, the word that you said…"
"Which cousin?" I ask, "I used to know your whole family."
"Well, she is not exactly a cousin, her sister is married to my
    brother-in-law's cousin.
She was in Thailand and bought beautiful carpets—"
"In Thailand? I never saw any."
"Well, maybe it was not Thailand, maybe it was Turkey, somewhere
    in Asia."

"What is for lunch?" she asks—
I had bought Zabars choice of the best—
Smoked Salmon: too salty,
fresh Herring salad: I make it better at home—
French cheese, Hungarian salami,
no no no Noooo, I would never touch such unhealthy food…
how about Cottage cheese, fresh yoghurt, 12 grain bread—fresh herbs?
"I make my own lunch," she suggests:
She needs all my kitchen gadgets, mostly those I do not have.
She chops and roasts, uses all my small plates,
Covers garlic bread from the baker with apple sauce, orange marmalade,
    topped with
fat-free, chemically treated Tofu—
crowned with Vanilla Yoghurt—
She did not offer to share it with me.
Disgusted she looks at my Israeli dish of red peppers, cucumber, radishes
    on dark bread,
"Would you like my freshly brewed cafecito—as they make it in Quito?"
"Oh no no noo, I would never drink that…
Oh, you take sugar on a grapefruit?"
She is horrified
NO NO NO—NEVER DO THAT
I get a lesson of how to wrap cheese, while I try to read to her the poems
    we learned in
school, in Vienna.
Der Erlkoenig, die Buergschaft, Heine, Rilke…
to build a bridge from this moment to the past
"I do not bother to waste time with that nonsense,

I gave away all my books, you should do the same, you have too many…"
"Your house should be neater, your car bigger,
your friends look shallow to me,
You dress not color coordinated—why don't you wear earrings,
no woman is dressed without earrings
no no no, noooo I would never go out unless the earrings match my shoes.
Why do you wear dresses instead of pants, nobody wears dresses anymore,
unless invited to a Gala.
When my sister was invited to the Gala of the sisterhood of…
no no no, noooo I was not invited, she was…
You do not keep spaghettis in a container of glass?
And all the berries closed hermetically, so no virus gets in,
Close the window, open the air conditioner, not too much, I get a cold, it
        is too hot."
And now comes the lauding of Fort Lauderdale:
never too hot, all the culture we need.

"I have to go to the doctor," I lie,
"Oh no no no, do not go now, we are having such a good time,
No no no nooo I would never leave a guest alone in the house!
Allegedly her doctor had said:
"Edith, now you are the most important person in your life."
Maybe in her own, but most certainly,
Never, ever again, in mine.

Arbeitsmoral

In meinem Kopf sind tausend Sonnenuntergaenge
Kirschblueten
Milchstrassen
und Glockenblumen
die auf Berg-Juniwiesen
ihren Beifall nicken.

Waere die Welt besser
wenn ich, zum, Beispiel
Kassenschraenke machte?
oder Schrauben
fuer Kisten,
die Bomben transportieren,
um daran zu profitieren?

Die Sonne scheint,
ich geh jetzt an den Strand
und werde dort, an Hand
von Listen und Statistik
das Thema Arbeitsmoral
studieren.

Oblivion

I love the word oblivion
I don't know what it means.
Is it a land
a dream
a flower or a wicked scheme?
the name of long forgotten love?
a tropic fruit?
an iron stove?

You can fall into this word
and forget,
or be forgotten
or forget the word.

Eine alte Frau packt…

Maerz 98

Erst die Pillen und die Brillen
alle Schluessel und die Schuh.
Die Rezepte und Adressen
nicht vergessen, welche Schuh?

Wo ist der Pass, wieso ist er nass?
Hotelschein, Flugschein, Fuehrerschein
und die roten Schuch hinein.

Die aufgesparten Dessous
vielleicht gibts mal ein Rendez vous
und darum, auf alle Faelle, die roten Schuh.

Naehzeug, Schreibzeug, Schwimmzeug, Turnzeug
Creme fuer Tag und Creme fuer Nacht
Haarshampoo und Fuessesalbe,
nimm die Ganze, nicht die Halbe,
Taschen, Flaschen, Schmuck, den Echten?

Jetzt die Blusen und die Jacken die muss man zusammen packen,
und die Flaschen in die Taschen, die Peruecke mit den Maschen,
Jetzt die Schals und Schreibpapier, alte Briefe lass ich hier,
Jupes und Kleider ganz zuletzt, dass die Reise sie nicht zerfetzt
halt, wo sind die roten Schuh!
Oh verflixt, das Telephon, das ist das Taxi, ich komm ja schon…

Angekommen, ausgepackt, alles da:
Brillen, Pillen, Schreibpapier,
Schals und Taschen, Plueschgetier
sechzehn Dosen und leere Flaschen,

Doch wo sind die Jupes und wo die Kleider,
alles zuhaus vergessen leider,
aber zum Glueck hab ich Dessous,
und vier Paar rote Schuh…

Nova Scotia

Baum und See
und See und Baum
und was anderes
sieht man kaum.

Wald und Wasser
Baum und Meer
und dafuer
komm soweit ich her?

Meer und Bucht
und Bucht am See
das ist alles
was ich seh.

Real secrets

Real secrets I only tell to myself.
Why should a friend, even the most trustworthy
Be a better keeper of my secrets
than I am myself.

I write a letter to myself especially
When the dark knights dance
their oppressive circle
enclosing me.

They throw heavy black velvet
over sun stars and flowers.
They cover everything with ashgrey cloth,
suffocating joy and pleasures.

I call up my defense army of joy of life,
The power of lust and laughter
When this poem to myself is finished
The clouds have passed.

An alle couch potatoes!

Du kannst das Foto einer Blume sehen
doch ihr Duft ist dir versagt.

Du kannst im Film auf Berge klettern,
doch wird der Wind nicht in deinen Haaren spielen.

Du kannst im Television
in, auf und unter allen Meeren schwimmen
doch deine Haut wird nie das Gefuehl des Wassers kennen.

Wenn du hungrig vor einer Auslage der feinsten Delikatessen
stehst
wirst du davon satt?

Madonna and the cell phones

Spring 2013

Three elderly elegant ladies sit on a bench
In a park under very old trees.
They admire and discuss a peaceful Madonna
when a cellular rings.
Is it mine, they ask each other
and begin to rummage in their bags.
The ring, of course, stops
Before any phone is produced.
Now they sit, Madonna forgotten
Each with a different model of cellular phone.
What is your number, Ursula asks,
Inge answers, I do not know,
But if I ring your phone, my number will appear on yours.
Wonderful idea, says Paula, hypnotizing hers,
As if the answer would appear magically on the screen.
So Inge calls Ursula, and her phone rings.
What do I do now, Ursula asks,
You press the green spot, says Paula, the youngest.
Which green spot? As Inge still let it ring,
Ursula's voice gets desperate.
They still sit in the park, under the very old trees,
In front of the peaceful Madonna.
Inge loses her patience, closes her phone, the ring stops.
Peace and quiet reigns.
Now, where is Inge's number?
they all press different buttons
On their particular phones.
A nun appears, with a stick in her hand.
Is she going to chastise us

As they do in religious schools
for not mastering the up-to-date high tech?
But the Nun just cleans the house of the Idol
Destroys invisible spidernets,
Cleans every impeccable clean corner
And quietly leaves.
Madonna seems worried,
Can she protect her peace
Against modern high tech?

Why do birds fly in a flock?

We are fragile precious antiques
To be handled with utmost care.
Now, we only have female friends
And expect from each other what only a mother
Gave, tender loving care.
We were spoiled by our husband and/or lovers
Whom we rewarded in the horizontal and we enjoyed orgasms
That made us ignore their negatives.
If we are lucky, giving, and tolerant
We fill the void with female friends,
try to support each other, ignore the fading health and strength.
We should not expect from each other what our mother or our men
    provided.
We cannot ask to be chauffeured, pampered and spoiled.
We should not be offended if we are not invited, we must avoid criticism,
    back stabbing or being witty
When it hurts.
Why do birds fly in a flock, and herds follow the alpha leader,
Because we are not solitary rocks, we need each other.

Three degrees

12. August 2011

There are three degrees of relationships:
Friends, acquaintances and
exchangeable people for shared activities.

A friend as in Schiller's Buergschaft (the pledge?)
You can call in the middle of the night
To bring you the spare key if you locked yourself out

Of your car or your house.
You trust him with your life,
your kids and even your bank account.

Acquaintances serve primarily for name dropping,
You use, sometimes abuse, each other to advance mutual
interests, to reach your, mostly vain, illusionary goals.

And then there are people with whom you play
tennis, golf, bridge or the market,
You like to hike with them, have the same subscription to football
or concerts.

      And they all are called friends.

There are three degrees of females: Ladies, women and yentes:

The ladies with whom you want to be seen
For networking or climbing the social ladder
are well dressed, well bred and cold as ice.

Women come in all qualities and shades,
they talk about prices, maids, children and grandchildren
And tales about their past, which often are untrue.

Yentes are amusing, they are the archetypes of bringing news
Gossip, rumors, they feel important if they report deaths, love affairs or
    secrets,
Just be careful not to appear in their repertoire.

      And they all are called friends.

There are three degrees of cars:
The one you drive, the one you dream of driving
And the one you tell your friends you drove,
Like a red Ferrari, when you hardly had the money for the bus.

There are three degrees of housekeepers:
the one who calls you by your first name,
Who loyally cleaned, cooked and dried your tears
For many years.

Or the one who comes, cleans and leaves.
But beware of #3, the one you think to be a friend,
but she just waits for the moment
to take revenge and denounces you with the IRS
or other authorities of power.

There are three degrees of hostesses:
The consumers, the collectors and those who make you feel safe and secure:
The consumers embrace every new face,
use its time, its energy for a short time,
then they discard them like a squeezed lime.

People collectors are eclectic, just the best will do
But once you are accepted to their inner circle,
You could consider them to be your friends forever.

Please introduce me to a #3,
the one who makes you feel safe and secure.
Remember, they are all called friends.

There are three degrees of victims:
those who fight back, because it is easier to die fighting than to be slaughtered
and those who enjoy and challenge to be victimized.
There must be something in between, please inform me if you know them.

There are three degrees of lovers:
Past, present and futures:
The past looked like Clark Gable
Was rich as Buffet, and loved you unconditionally. He always died a
　　tragic death.
Present and future depend on
your age, luck, looks and what you bring to the bed and to the table.

Nature and Time

Ki ilu—as if

Jan, 5th 2010

(Ki-ilu: this magical word rules life in Israel whatever happens
Theatre, concerts, parties, parades, meetings, are not cancelled)

Here in America we live ki ilu our planet were safe and secure
That we have enough food water gas and oxygen for sure
As if hungry masses did not lurk to destroy
Our fragile precious web of capitalistic joy.
Ki ilu Islamic terrorists were a children's story
They could never harm this nation's glory.
Ki ilu our whole species has learned to control
Our deadly instinct for fratricide war,
Therefore I want a new man a true man a macho man
he can be young or old, but should have a heart of,
and his pockets full of, gold.
He should love laughter lust and whatever I write
When I need him he should never be out of my sight
But when I need my space he should have the flair
To immediately disappear into thin air.
With him, like all of us, I shall swim in the vat of milk,
until we sit on butter, as Aesop did think.
Ki ilu we were young and our love like hot steam
And I live, ki ilu, I never abandon this dream.

Faceless

My mother sank into the ocean of time
so did my friends, my country
and I.
That which walks
with my name
and my faec
is not
I.
I am surprised
when somebody greets me on the street—
does that mean
one can recognize
Me?

My child has gone
to a far, strange land
married a stranger
talks a strange tongue
is estranged
from me.

But:
as long as I throw
a shadow in the Sun
and in a mirror
I see a reflection
of my face
I know,
somewhere
there is still
a little
I.

Skidmore Metaphors

She is like a leaf in the wind
where ever it blows she will fly
She is a dandelion, white lace, round and ripe
You blow on it, it disperses its beauty in hundreds of tiny parachutes.

She is a sponge, absorbing and needing and taking
And only returns what she got
when you really squeeze her hard.

She is like a carnivorous flower
She has no problem to attract and enchant
But most men sense the danger and escape
As fast and as far as they can.

She is like a woman
But nature has failed to fill her
with sweetness and nurturing strength
And all the chocolate she needs cannot fill this void.

Ersatz.

du kannst das Foto einer Blume sehen,
doch ihr Duft ist dir versagt.
du kannst im Film auf Berge klettern,
doch der Wind wird nicht in deinen Haaren spielen.
du kannst, im Television, in, auf und unter allen Meeren schwimmen
doch deine Haut wird nie das Gefuehl des Wasser's kennen.
wenn du hungrig vor einer Auslage die feinsten Delikatessen siehst:
wirst du davon satt?

Herbst

Tritt ein in den Dom des Herbstes
und fasse die flammenden Farben
mit dem Ohr
wie einen Chor
den ein prachtliebender Fuerst der Renaissance
in Auftrag gab.
Sieh, eine Tapisserie
gewoben und gestickt
aus Millionen Blaettern zusammengeflickt
Das Rot des Feuers
zum Braun der Bronze
Kupfer, Messing und Gold
nichts ist zu teuer
fuer diese Pracht
als Symbol der Macht.

Es klagt der Wald: bald bin ich arm, kahl, alt, und kalt
doch komme ich wieder in Fruehlingspracht
glaubt an mich wie an den Dom
der Asyl und Hoffnung gibt in Zeiten von Not.
In der nackten Not steckt schon der Fruehling
und im Fruehling klingt die Symphonie vom Herbst.

Univers-Gebet

Ich bin Gott in meinem Univers
Und eine winzige Zelle in seinem.
So wie er habe ich Macht
zu erschaffen,
Doch Vieles folgt den ewigen Gesetzen,
Dessen winzige Zelle SEIN Univers ist.

Ich hoere Gebete meiner Zellen
Erhoere sie, nur so existiere Ich.
Gilt das Gleiche fuer IHN?

Spaziergang mit Kurt

12.Sept. 88

Ich seh die Blaetter fallen
die ich als Knospe gekannt
die Aepfel reifen am Baume
die gestern in Bluete ich fand.

Die Kinder, denen ich Pate stand
sind heute erwachsene Leute.
Nur ich selbst bin jung
und hungrig nach Beute,
nach Liebe, Erleben
und Allem
das mich mein Lebenlang freute.

Es ist so vieles schon Vergangenheit

Es ist so vieles schon Vergangenheit
das kuerzlich noch so wichtig war.
Soviel getan, gehoert, gesehen
so viele Menschen haben meinen Weg gekreuzt
nur wenig Freundschaft blieb davon bestehn.

Obwohl sich vieles wiederholt,
ist es unmoeglich einen Gluecksmoment zu wiederholen
Der Flieder, der einst lieblich duftete, die Mondscheinnacht, ein
      Apfelbaum in Bluete
zuerst bejubelt es die Jugend
das Mannesalter uebersiehts.
Im Alter, weil es sich so automatisch wiederholt
und trotzdem nie wieder ist, wie es mal war,
macht es uns traurig
und verleitet uns zum dichten.

Zeit

Tage jagen
Stunden daemmern
Sekunden sind helle
wie Licht　　　　　　　　(oder: Sekunden sind helles Licht)

Jahre fliegen
Aber Minuten wiegen
Wie Ewigkeits-Pflicht

Jahrzehnte verschmelzen
Momente sind jetzt,
Momente, die laengst vergangen,
erstehen wieder,
Anfang wird Ende
Der Kreis wird sich schliessen…

Cultural conditioning

Mein Kind, vergiss nie,
dass du seit Jahrmillionen
gewoehnt bist, in Natur zu wohnen.
Du bist konditioniert
an kristall-klar-kalten Tagen
in Waeldern dir Nahrung zu erjagen.

Liebessehnsucht wird in dir entstehen
wenn linde Luefte
leicht in Lindenblueten wehen.

Du wirst voll Eile Vieh und Heu beschuetzen wollen,
wenn dunkle Wolken,
drohendes Gewitter, grollen.
Sogar wenn du noch nie Kuh oder Korn getastet,
Ur instinkte sinds, die dein Gehaben ueberlastet.

Wind

Ich liebe Dich, Wind
Du bist Bewegung
Du bringst Erregung

Ich bin wie Du
wild, sanft,
immer frei
gehoere nur
der Natur.

Emigration and Depression

Ich seh' meinen Schatten

Spaziergang im Central Park, 7 Uhr Frueh,
am Tag der Hochzeit, Marion und Gregg.

Ich seh' meinen Schatten
und mein Schatten ist alt.
Der Ruecken rund
die Schultern gebeugt,
der Kopf geneigt
und die Augen, die man im Schatten nicht sieht,
verheult.

Der Gang ist wankend
und bei jedem Schritt den der zoegernde Fuss macht,
zittert der ganze Koerper mit.
die Seele ist jung, so glaubt sie
mit dem Leben und Streben
und Geben und Weben
mit Musik und Sport
mit Wandern und Tanzen
so glaubt sie
Schritt zu halten.

Doch der Schatten ist alt. Und der Gang hat Falten.

Beweint mich nicht...

Beweint mich nicht,
wenn ich an meinem Uebermut
krepier.
Und klagt nicht
wir haben's ihr gesagt,
wozu hat sie's gewagt?

muss man tatsaechlich mit 60 Jahren
in Karate Klassen
mit Teenagern sich schlagen?

Sich in Seen, Bergen, Meeren
viel zu weit hinaus sich wagen?
sich in Aerobic, Disco, und Taebo
wie ein Derwisch herumzujagen,
Ihr habt das Recht zu sagen:
Sie krepierte, weil sie ihr Alter ignorierte.

Es war tatsaechlich reiner Uebermut,
aber immerhin
es war MUT
und es war gut.

The blues.

Wie oft schon sah ich auf eine schlafende Stadt
sah die Lichter unter mir funkeln.
Da bin ich, da bleib ich, da bin ich Zu haus,
hier kann man noch leben, so dacht ich.

Zuerst in Wien, vom Kahlenberg aus,
die Donau, der Stefel, mein Haus,
dann kamen die Nazis, wir wurden verjagt,
und mit Wien war es also ganz aus.

Dann stand ich am Bre, in Lugano,
der Lago und die Trauben so blau,
der Salvatore, Campione, Vanini,
aber das Leben war leer und flau.

Also dann nach Zürich, vom Uetliberg ein Blick wie im Traum,
im Osten Gebirge, unten die Stadt um den See drapiert.
Doch Zurich ist einsam,
also zieh weiter…

Und dann Tel Aviv, Kein Berg in der Naeh,
doch von Haifa vom Carmel ein Blick:
Das Meer so blau und die Stadt fast wie Zürich,
von oben nur, allerdings.

Israel ist eng. so gehts nach New York, auch da ist kein Berg in der Naehe.
Doch wohn ich am 31. Stock, und vom Fenster aus schau ich und sehe:
den Park und die Oper, das Plaza und mehr,
doch leider auch sehr viel Verkehr.

Jetzt bin ich in Quito, und der Himmel ist blau,
vom Panecillo aus sieht man die Stadt.
Die Kirchen, die Plazas, und oh Schreck,
auch Wolkenkratzer, Verkehr und viel Dreck.

Von wo ich auch schau, mal ist der Himmel blau,
mal das Meer, mal ein See, und meistens ich.
Wo bin ich, wo bleib ich, wo bin ich zu Haus?
Wo kann ich noch leben? so frag ich…

Where I Am From: True or Untrue

I was born in the city where the Danube is blue
The heart of its citizen is golden
And they waltz day and night through.
　　Untrue
The Danube is dirty
The people are cruel
And they dance reggae and hip hop
Like in New York.

My ancestors came as scribes with the Romans
To Vindobona—where the wine is good
Which is called Vienna today
And wine still is the main staple.
　　All of the above is true

They were cloister Jews, serfs to the monks of Melk,
During dangerous times like the crusades
They were protected inside the cloister walls.
In return the men made money for the monks
By doing their dealings and wheelings.
While the girls served inside the cloister
In kitchens and gardens and other locations,
Hence my blue eyes and natural blond hair.
　　All of the above is true.

When Joseph the Second
Whom you know from "Amadeus"
Gave the Jews all civil rights in 1780
The Ghettos were opened,
My ancestors moved to and around Vienna
Until we were kicked out in 1938.

One grandmother recited Goethe, Schiller and Heine
As my lullabies.
The others were farmers
And when a thunderstorm brews
I have the urge to protect cattle and hay under a roof
Although in New York I have neither cattle nor fields.
    All of the above is true.

     —Inge Ginsberg

Ode to my white knight

Du vertreibt die Drachen der Angst und der Furcht
Du hebst mich zu dir auf das Pferd der Hoffnung
Du verteidigst das Leben bis zur hoechsten Instanz
Du bist stets zur Hand und bereit
einzutreten in den oft verzweifelten Kampf
Du feiner kleiner weisser Ritter
Winzig zwar doch unersetzlich
Mein Zoloft!

Muttertag

Mein Muttertag ist einsam und leer
meine Kinder hab ich gemordet
als Foetusse trieb ich sie ins Meer
drum ist mein Muttertag einsam und schwer.

Mein Muttertag ist einsam und kalt
aus Feigheit und Faulheit trieb ich sie ab.
die nichtigsten Nichtigkeiten schienen mir wichtig
jetzt bin ich, am Muttertag, einsam und alt.

Heute, am Muttertag, waeren die Vier hier mit mir.
Sie waeren nicht alle Genies.
Aber ihr Leben haette ich ihnen gegeben
anstatt der Trauer ueber 4 Morde in mir.

Emigration

Das Schlimmste war das Entwurzeln
wir sprechen viele Sprachen
und alle mit falschem Accent
das Klima passt uns nirgends
die Haurtfarbe und Gerueche der Nachbarn sind fremd.

Wir wandern in vielen Laendern
ohne Wurzeln, Ziel und Zweck
Unsere Telefon und Reisespesen
fressen den Loewenanteil des Budgets weg.

Und doch muessen wirs geben
um Freunde und Kinder zu sehen,
und um nicht sie zu verlieren
im Meer von Raum und Zeit.

Foolish Heart

Andaman beach, February 2002

Foolish heart
Shall I laud you or curse you?
Laud you
For still wishing and hoping
Wanting desiring,
Still beating to loyal and regular drums

Or curse you
For still wishing and hoping
And aching for
"La feria de la fruta"
Illusions
Over and over again,
Still beating to loyal and regular drums

Keeping this mini Universe
Alive
Its mission not yet fulfilled
To see and describe
The wonders and beauty all around
Protect it from destruction
Still not knowing How

As long as there is pain
healing is near
Self releasing and relying
on nothing but the Universe
Within and around,
Wise heart
Still beating to loyal and regular drums.

I'll start my life tomorrow

"I'll start my life tomorrow"
Is a very cheap Terutz—excuse!

I started my life
A long time ago.

I do, and always did
What I wanted to do

NOBODY, NOTHING NEVER
EVER COULD STOP ME,

Not even being tired
or sick like now

I drink two more espressos
Take antibiotic, if needed.

And on I go, like a candle
Burning at both ends.

I still have to listen to so much music,
Read books, enjoy nature and love,

There is friendships and learning
And exercise class.

There are kisses and frocks
And trips and rhymes

as Dorothy Parker said:
they do not fill my heart, but still they fill my time.

D. Parker.
My candle burns at both ends
It cannot last the night
And ah my friends and ah my foes
It makes a lovely light.

Valentine's Day Song

to our friends
1995?

This is a valentines song for you
and what I say is really true
friends like you are hard to find
loyal, honest, good and kind.

A chewreh is a group of friends
once you belong it never ends
support and help in case of need
or celebrate joys and fortify creed.

Always in search of something new
we share teachers and their due
we study, discuss, we read and learn
to fight off old age at every turn.

We feed each others needs and longings
we share our homes, time and belongings
for many more years we all should stay
just as we are, happy valentine's day.

2004
And what I said was never true
You lied to me as I lied to you
However, when the friends were gone
It is unbearable to be alone.

Depression

Die schwarzen Teufel tanzen wieder
und werfen ihren schweren Samt
in Schwaden ueber meine welken, mueden Glieder

Tanz mit, sagt Kurt
den Tanz von ungesuehnter Schuld
der nicht real, doch umso
schwerer liegt auf meiner Leber
das "haett ich doch," "wie schad, zu spaet,"—
vergiss die Pille nicht, sagt Kurt.

Die schwarzen Teufel tanzen wieder ihren Reigen
sie verdunkeln die Sonne
und zerfressen den Mond.
die gesichter von Freunden zeigen
sich in ihren hoehnischen Masken,
so dass ein Wiedersehen kaum noch lohnt.
Das Plus und die Blessings sind vergessen
ich zaehl nur die flops, Kishalon,
la Chamade,
was gut ist, ist schlecht, und was schlecht ist, noch schlechter,
es lohnt kaum noch etwas,
nicht mal das Vergessen.

Tanz mit, sagt Kurt, den Tanz der Depression.
doch vergiss Dein Zoloft nicht…

Zum Schaden noch den Spott.
Das Sublimieren von Leid und Weh
das Dichter, Maler, Kuenstler durch
Jahrhunderte zu ungeahnten Leistungen

inspiriert
wird durch ein paar Milli—milligramm
Seratonin besiegt.
Haetten Heine, Rilke, Kafka, Michelangelo,
Leonardeo, Dante, praktisch alle
Prozac gekannt und konsumiert
sie waeren harmlos gluecklicher gewesen,
doch wir, die Welt, die Nachwelt,
sehr viel aermer…

Ode to my daughter and my granddaughter

Zurich 14.6.2011

Thank you for doing nothing for me
Forcing me to be independent
To think and to pack
To pay and to check:
The bills and the statements
And balance the checks
To rent and collect the rents
To be sure all insurances are paid
and that the insurances pay any damage.

I went to St. Petersburg for the first time,
I booked the flight and went to Berne for the Visa
Shortly after I rented a car, a shift, and drove to Grindelwald
And the Giessbachfaelle, steep narrow mountain roads,
Just to prove: I can do it.

A housewife's chores are never done
An independent woman's agenda is full
Still, there is time to walk and to talk
And yes, to write about all of the above.

Lohnt es noch

(Abwehr der tiefen Depression 17.11.11)

Ich kann gehen, stehen, sprechen, essen, lesen
Ich kan lachen, Gedichte machen
kramen in alten Sachen,
da finde ich alte Briefe,
denke an heisse Lieben
Fuehle noch die Hitze
heisser Naechte
Und exotischer Reisen,
Ich singe leise altvertraute Weisen,
Ich kann mir teure Theaterkarten leisten,
Ohne in der Schlange zu warten,
Ich sehe das neueste Musical auf VIP Sitze.
Ich kann hoeren,
die Musik der grossen Meister
und der Baeume Rauschen
kann ich noch immer lauschen.

Und vergiss nicht deine groesste Freiheit,
NOCH entscheide ich, ganz allein
ueber meine Zeit.

Prau Pulte See in Films.

(1980?)

Mein Kind, erinnerst du dich an den Prau Pulte See?
Der Weg fuehrt sanft bergab
durch dichten alten Wald
der in vollen Farben duftet.
Der Weg war ideal, denn du warst klein
und die zwei Tanten aus Grenoble waren alt.

Du hattest Keuchhusten.
Es war noch vor der Zeit
als Impfung dem Kinderzimmer all die Schrecken nahm
die uns bedrohten.
Als jeder Schnupfen vielleicht Beginnn von Kinderlaehmung war
und Masern zu Meningitis und Verbloedung fuehren konnten.
Es ist schon lange her, denn
du bist heute eine Dame mittleren Alters,
Archaeologin, die eben jezt in China
nach Tonsoldaten graebt.

Ich ging heute zum Prau Pulte see
Allein.
die Tanten sind schon lange tot und du bist sehr weit weg.

Noch immer ist der Wald
uralt,
der Weg fuehrt sanft bergab, und jezt, gleich nach der letzten Biegung
wird mir smaragdener See entgegenleuchten,
alte Nymphenmaerchen bewachen
sein tiefgruenes Geheimnis.

Wann immer wir zum See kamen
hat seine Schoenheit dir jubelndes Freudekraehn entlockt
waehrend die 2 Tanten leise seufzten.
Heute versteh ich, dass sie der eigenen Jugend gedachten
versaeumte Romantik
ungelebtes Lieben, ungeliebtes Leben.

Noch eine Biegung rund um einen dick verknorrten Stamm:
ich erstarre vor Schreck
der See ist weg.
Eine hohle Grube voller Sand,
nicht mal sehr tief, enthaelt verstreute tote Struenke.
Man hoert Haemmern und nahe Autos.

Mir kommt der Film "der Planet der Affen" in den Sinn
als die Menschen unsere schoene Welt total zerstoerten.
Sind wir schon so weit? sind wir dem Ende schon so nah?

Messages by Inge Ginsberg

The Manifest of a Mini Universe: Think

June 15th 2007

The message was heard in the whole small universe: "If we want to exist our predestinated time, order and harmony have to be restored ot the programmed quality. We can only survive if every one, from the highest to the lowest, does his duty. This message is sent from the highest authority." A hectic realignment, reorganization, reconsideration of respective duties of every group was proof of obedience and the collective wish to continue their existence of joy and pleasure.

Except one: one of the lowliest, farthest down in the hierarchy was tired of his environment. He was almost always in the dark, surrounded by unpleasant odors and sounds, often hot, humid, slithery, he had the notion that there must be something bigger, better out there, more than just get food, the minimum of air and the constant fight against the arch enemy, aliens who try to squeeze into the already tight quarters, who are strong and sly, contribute nothing to the community, changing its ways and even color.

With all his force and superior intelligence he found his way out, found a rushing stream to take him up, as fast as he never dreamed, he passed never imagined forms and life forms, similar to himself but much higher developed, performing the most complicated functions, cooperating in minute activities, some produced something, some transported it, some changed or exchanged it, in perfectly orchestrated speed. But still that was not the vision the little guy was searching for. He changed venues, passed more complicated organizations, under the cover of being small, tough and unimportant he reached the highest regions, the light became unbearable, and through a huge, ,black opening he looked into dimensions he could not grasp, forms and colors, width and farness, of gigantic geometric structures, and he heard a sound of heavenly harmony, the same he had often heard faint and far, now he was in it himself, he was in the light, he had a glimpse of creation. Happily he went on, first into the dark, then into the red rush, where the defense organization detected and annihilated him.

He was one cell of the toenail of a human body. He was tired of living within shoes, fighting the nail fungus. The human body, which was his universe, only felt an irritation in the eye while meditating to live to 120 years, and listening to his favorite background music.

For the toe nail cell with a visionary intelligence, this body was the universe.

Maybe I am one cell of a bigger body. My universe, also called God.

The Story of the Peacock Who Was In Love with Himself
An anti-Darwin story

The peacock showed his beautiful tail, he spread it wide, he danced to the right, he pranced to the left, he shook his shiny feathers and vibrated with all his force.

Soon, three peahens arrived, attracted by the graceful dance. They showed their feathers, wiggled to the right, danced to the left, vibrated their modest tail, waiting for the happy moment.

But the peacock ignored them. He continued to play and to display and forgot why Nature had given him his beauty. He desperately tried to see his own tail. Faintly he remembered that, a long time ago in the far-far land of India, his forefathers had the honour to be the vehicle for Sarasvati, the Goddess of music. The goddess stroked their feathers like a harp, while they were flying over land and sea. But one of his forefathers became too proud and disobedient, he refused to bend his head to the ground when the goddess wanted to play with his feathers, while they were not flying. The goddess became very angry and punished the peacock and all his offspring: "Nevermore will you see your own beauty, as hard as you may try!"

Many, many years have passed, this peacock lived far away from India, he never knew anything about the Goddess of music or the punishment. Obstinate and vain, exactly as was his forefather, he continued his solitary dance. The three peahens resigned and sadly returned to their corner, waiting.

But soon another peacock arrived. He did not display his feathers, because he did not have any, only two or three sad little brushes were trailing in the sand. Was he too young or too old? The peahens did not care. One after the other joined him in a short but fruitful dance. Proudly, the ugly peacock walked away, satisfied the three peahens enjoyed the sun.

The vain peacock was still dancing with himself, soon got tired, folded and dropped his fine equipment, sadly all the unusued beauty fell to the ground, all the shiny peacock feathers, every one with a shiny blue eye, they all became just a dusty, useless mess in the sand.

Bored and lonely, the vain peacock stood, while shade was slowly embracing him.

Two Limericks

Lyme

Oct. 1 09

I have a disease called Lyme
The four letter words I want to use don't rhyme
It affected my heart
Which might need a pacemaker to start
And it steals my most precious commodity: my time.

Benalcazar
1498-1552

Conquistador, founder of cities and the Panamerican Highway, visionary of combining the Spanish and the Inca culture in peace. His biography of 300 pages told in 5 lines.

There was a Jewish boy from Spain
Who fled to the New World in vain
He conquered the Incas
Gave all their land and gold to his king, as
His kids and he by the Inquisition were slain.

The ship of sheep

August 2014

The luxury deck,
where the power people
stay and play
Is called Ukraine.
As in 1914, or later 1936 in Spain
Strength versus tolerance
is tested,
while the captain plays golf.

The first class deck, called Israel
is always in the news.
Although the numbers are small
Negative publicity is widespread.
The first lieutenant, Kerry,
tries hard, but does not convince
and does not achieve.
And the captain plays golf.

Right in the captain's quarters, called Ferguson
While he is absent,
Steam builds up among the crew.
Many big upheavals
have started like that
Endangering ship, destination
and the upper decks.

The second deck, called Isis,
is the most dangerous.
Only 30,000 victims
have to be saved.
Nobody has heard of them before,
Negligence and lethargy had allowed them on the ship,
Obvious to everybody, except to the captain
Who does not realize,
that this might be the trigger point,
the critical mass
setting the whole ship on fire.

In the machine room, called Syria,
A fight goes on for three years among the crew,
brother against brother.
The captain favors the destabilizing group
He endangers the supply of oil.
He betrays the chief engineer, (Assad),
who despite his threats
Has kept quiet, order and peace
in that whole area.

The captain should be aware that the group he ignores
Is the most dangerous.
Organized in small opaque cells,
Brainwashed, sex deprived youth
fanatically death adoring
as they expect 72 virgins waiting for them.

They are dangerous as cancer cells
As contagious as Ebola once they grab the power.
Nothing decisive is decided
No protection will protect the ship
If the captain plays golf instead of leads.

Poor Jim Foley might still have his head on his shoulders
If the captain had been at his wheel
To make the decisive decision,
For which he is highly paid.
All actions to save poor Jim Foley
Came a little bit too late
because the captain was standing between two holes
instead of standing at his wheel.

The latest most stupid thing to admit
That there is no strategy or plan
To protect the ship
That floats without leadership on the Ocean
A ghost ship, still believing in its strength
That is totally gone.
The captain stands in shoes much too big for his feet
Too big for him to walk or over obstacles to leap.

AND THIS IS THE STATUS OF THE SHIP OF SHEEP
AUGUST 2014.

Lamento

by Inge, Michelangelo, Goethe, and Rilke

Michelangela klagte: Oh Gott.
warum hast du die Seele
eines schoenen junges Mannes
In den Körper dieses haesslichen Krueppels gesteckt.

Auch ich klage:
Die schöne heissbluetige junge Frau
Ist jetzt in dem zerfallenden, stinkenden
Verfleckten Koerper versteckt.

Von der her, sendet sie
Mit fliehenden Kraeften
Verzweifelte Rufe nach Liebe, nach Waerme,
Ohne die sie verreckt.

Oh Herr, mein Leben war sehr gross
Schick mir noch ein Mal
einen warmen Maennerkoerper
und in dieser Liebe lass die Suesse los.

Befiehl den Seelen, reif zu sein,
schick ihnen noch ein paar suedlichere Tage
lass sie sich ein Haus bauen, um nicht allein zu sein,
wenn auch der Herbst vergeht.

Diebstahl Anzeige

Tel Aviv 12.4.14

In den Waeldern rund um Jerusalem blueh'n die Rakafot (Zyklamen),
Und ich habe sie nicht gesehen.
Am Golan weht der Bergwind vom Hermon,
Und ich habe ihn nicht geatmet.

In Hamat Gader, im teueren Privat teil
Fliesst das heilende Wasser,
Das meine Schmerzen lindert
Und ich konnte es nicht erreichen.

Den Sonnenuntergang hinter dem Meer
Die schoene Stunde, den kuehlen Wind,
Spielte ich Bridge mit andernen einsamen
Alten verzweifelten Damen.

Meine echten guten alten Freunde
In diversen Alterscheimen verstreut
Doch konnte ich sie nicht besuchen,
Einander danken fuer treue loyale Freundschaft.

Nur gemeinsam kann man sich erinnern:
an die tollen Feste, wir tanzten bis zum Fruehstueck,
und dann in unseren Abendkleidern ans Meer,
wo der Strand nur aus Sand bestand

im Sonnenaufgang badeten wir nackt miteinander.
Telefonisch klingen diese Bilder banal.
Auch nur Telefon mit den Freunden
im Kibbutz im noerdlichsten Norden

Wo bis 1967 die Syrer auf die Kinder schossen,
Heute schiessen sie auf ihre eigenen.
In den Wiesen und Feldern im Galil
nicken die feueroten Kalaniot (Mohnblumen)

und ich kann nicht zurück nicken.
Die grossen Flächen in Gelb, Mimosen, Ginster,
Kleine Savionim
In der Stadt gibt es nur kleine Bueschel in vergessenen Gaertchen.

Das alles wurde mir gestohlen.
Ich bitte um Wiedergutmachung.

Count Your Blessings

21. Juni 81

I live in a land that I hate
I lose all the money I have made
my daughter sails the Seven Seas
my husband wants to get rid of me
Cancer in me waits to attack
I am either fat or a nervous wreck
my real friends are dead or far away
you tell me:
will I ever have a happy day?

Poems not by Inge Ginsberg

Traenen
by NINI

eine traene begann zu fliessen
und macht sich auf ihren weg.
traenen wissen wenn sie fliessen
ist es oftmals schon zu spaet.

allerdings besteht die hoffnung,
dass ein traenenmeer entsteht,
sodas niemals eine traene ungeliebt verloren geht.

10. Juli 2012

Auf Wiedersehen
by NINI

aufwiedersehen ist leicht gesagt,
aufwiedersehen ist oftmals hart,
aufwiedersehen birgt bangen,
aufwiedersehen ist oft befangen,
aufwiedersehn bringt glueck,
aufwiedersehen macht auch verrueckt,
aufwiedershen heisst bis bald,
aufwiedersehen kennt keine gewalt.

22. August 2012

Ich will dir nicht gefallen
by NINI

Ich will dir nicht gefallen, mich duengt zu streiten mit dir.
Erst dann wirst du erkennen welch geist ruht in mir.
Die spiele des lebens moegen kommen, getarnt durch luege
und zier.

du allerdings wirst sie begreifen und spielst sie mit plesier.
drum wahre das edle und den klaren geist, denn er ist es
der dich schuetzt und und gleichzeitig befreit.

30. Juni 2012

Lightning Source UK Ltd.
Milton Keynes UK
UKHW041039180219
337530UK00001B/25/P